KU-470-468

THE DAILY MALE

THE DAILY MALE

Nick Battle

Authentic

MILTON KEYNES ● COLORADO SPRINGS ● HYDERABAD

Copyright © 2008 Nick Battle

14 13 12 11 10 09 08   7 6 5 4 3 2 1

First published 2008 by Authentic Media
9 Holdom Avenue, Bletchley, Milton Keynes, Bucks, MK1 1QR, UK
1820 Jet Stream Drive, Colorado Springs, CO 80921, USA
OM Authentic Media, Medchal Road, Jeedimetla Village,
Secunderabad 500 055, A.P., India
www.authenticmedia.co.uk

Authentic Media is a division of IBS-STL U.K., limited by guarantee, with its
Registered Office at Kingstown Broadway, Carlisle, Cumbria, CA3 0HA.
Registered in England & Wales No. 1216232. Registered charity 270162

The right of Nick Battle to be identified as the Author of this Work has been
asserted by him in accordance with the Copyright, Designs and Patents Act 1988.

All rights reserved. No part of this publication may be reproduced, stored in a
retrieval system, or transmitted in any form or by any means, electronic, mechanical,
photocopying, recording or otherwise, without the prior permission of the publisher
or a licence permitting restricted copying. In the UK such licences are issued by the
Copyright Licensing Agency, 90 Tottenham Court Road, London, W1P 9HE

British Library Cataloguing in Publication Data
A catalogue record for this book is available from the British Library

ISBN-13: 978-1-86024-702-6

Scripture quotations are taken from the *Holy Bible*, New Living Translation,
copyright © 1996, 2004. Used by permission of Tyndale House Publishers, Inc.,
Carol Stream, Illinois 60188, USA. All rights reserved.

Excerpt taken from the song 'Money' by Roger Waters.
Copyright © 1973 Warner/Chappell. Used by permission.

Excerpt taken from the song 'Don't Feel Your Touch' by Bruce Cockburn.
Copyright © 1988 Golden Mountain Music Corp. (Socan). Used by permission.

Excerpt taken from the song 'If You Can't Shout Saved' by Ian Smale & Dave P. Evans.
Copyright © 1979 Thankyou Music. Adm. by worshiptogether.com songs excl. UK &
Europe, adm. by kingswaysongs.com tym@kingsway.co.uk. Used by permission.

Excerpt taken from the song 'Muscle Culture' by Steve Fairnie & Steve Rowles.
Copyright © 1979 Onward Music Ltd. Used by permission.

Cover Design by Norman Trotter
Cover photo by Lauren Mitton
Print Management by Adare
Printed and bound in Great Britain by J.H. Haynes & Co., Sparkford

For my godparents, Arthur and Shirley Hartup.

Contents

Thanks

I would like to thank the following people for a whole bunch of different reasons.

My publisher Malcolm Down for his wisdom, humour and grace in once again managing me through the writing process. He is a remarkable man endowed with endless patience and wonderful diplomatic skills!

Everyone at Authentic Media and STL who do so much to further the Good News that is Jesus.

Clive Price who has become a friend in the process of editing my ramblings and whose contributions to 'Nick's notes' have been important.

I would also like to thank my mentor and friend J.John and his wife Killy and sons Michael, Simeon and Ben for their consistent, loving friendship.

Not forgetting all those who pray for us as a family and for Gravel Road Ministries.

My two gorgeous daughters Misha and Jodie who I embarrass with alarming regularity.

And my dear wife Nicky who carries our precious gift from God due to be released round about the same time as this book.

To God be the glory.

Acknowledgements

I would like to thank Roger Waters for his kind permission in letting me use the lyric from the Pink Floyd classic, 'Money', and in particular Kate Watkins and Mark Fenwick from his management office who took the time to facilitate this.

Thanks also go to Ishmael and the estate of the late Dr Martyn Lloyd-Jones for allowing me to use some of the pearls they have dropped along the gravel road.

Introduction

I actually wanted to write something to make you laugh – not necessarily cry (unless they're tears of joy!). And during the writing process, I've discovered just how grumpy I can be.

From my lofty perspective after 50 years on this planet, I'd like to rant about a few things that tick me off – and work out why they're so annoying. I'd like to make you smile, and offer a spiritual view on those things that drive us all completely nuts.

I've about 25 years left on this gravel road – if I'm a very good boy – so I need to do this. And I need to do it now. I want to talk about love, laughter and faith for as long as I'm allowed to keep the pedal to the metal.

So thanks for buying this book. Get out of the fast lane, put your feet up, grab a digestive and a cup of tea and get ready to exercise your chuckle muscle.

Time to love, laugh and live.

Nick Battle
Chorleywood, England
January 2008

1

MY BODY IS A TEMPLE

'There are some advantages to growing old my friends.'
(Dr Martyn Lloyd-Jones)

I told a friend the other day that my body was a temple. Quick as a flash, he responded, 'Yes, I know – the Acropolis!'

When I was young and regularly humping my own musical equipment around this sceptred isle, I had a body that would've made Tom Cruise envious. I could eat what I wanted, when I wanted, drink real ale, eat pizza for England, and still not be possessed of an ounce of fat. Now, instead of a six-pack, my stomach's like a keg of Watneys Party-Seven.

Why do we have to deteriorate as we get older? It's such a shame, ironic even. But the unwritten law of the male universe says that as we become wiser, we seem to become wider.

Tonsorially challenged, I have learned to live with the 'M effect' at the front of what used to be my hairline. But imagine my dismay when my daughters pointed out I was now also developing a large 'O' where the crown of my hair used to be. Pretty soon I will resemble a Buddhist monk, who instead of chanting, 'Om' will be shouting 'Mo!'.

Surprisingly(!), I used to be vain. I'd spend hours in front of the mirror practising my poses – not with a tennis racket – but with my guitar. I would study my reflection carefully as I pouted and preened. Now the only time I look at myself is when I shave, and even then with great reluctance, as these days the only familiar facets of my face are my eyes. Gone is the tight jawline, unblemished skin, boyish innocence. In their place is a visage that suggests I might have lived a little – or a lot. There is sun damage, a certain jowliness that suggests too many fine wines and fine foods – and my stubble is more stubborn than ever. And yet we're told men get 'more attractive as they get older'.

Surprisingly(!) I used to be vain

I have friends, showbiz mates, who have gone under the knife, some once, others regularly. But I could never take the pain. And though I wouldn't want to judge them on the issue, I really don't want to mess with the little bits God has given me.

Yet at the same time as physically everything starts to head south, spiritually maybe we become more aware of the finishing tape. Just what do we think we're doing in this mad race of life? What *really* are our priorities?

Hopefully we'll spend more time with our loved ones, investing in their future. Gently trying to raise the bar for future generations. Get stuck in to our communities, churches even. Try to make a difference for as long as God allows.

But I'm **pregnant** with **hope**

Sometimes I feel like life on this earth is a prolonged gestation period – with the real birth taking place when, one day, we look into God's eyes.

Am I pregnant? Well I am a chubby 50-year-old, and perhaps the answer is yes. It certainly *looks* like there's a baby in there.

But I'm pregnant with hope. The hope of a future. The hope that I can achieve what God wants me to – in the time left. And the promise of heaven.

NICK'S NOTES THINGS TO DO

✔ EAT A FEW LESS PIZZAS

✔ DRINK A BIT LESS WINE

✔ WALK (NOT DRIVE) TO THE SHOPS

✔ SPEND MORE TIME WITH THE FAMILY

2

THE ROAD TO HELL

It's 1960. My mother is wheeling me in (in a good old pram, not one of these new-fangled, custom-designed, wind-tunnel-tested baby travelling systems) to Manchester's Free Trade Hall. Sir John Barbirolli is conducting The Hallé Orchestra for a concert that is being broadcast live on the BBC. They're playing Tchaikovsky's *1812 Overture*.

I'm only three. Yet I sit enraptured by the whole experience. That is, until the timpani and cymbals explode into life. I howl the whole place down. My mother quickly exits with me, as the more seriously minded classicists frown at her over their music scores like a herd of hippopotamuses with hiatus hernias. How dare this woman distract them from assiduously following every nuance of this wonderful work?

Noise annoys.

Cut to Nether Green Junior School, Sheffield, 6 years later. I am sitting on the stage with two huge cymbals in my hands as the choir sing *Rule Britannia*. This time it's my turn to make an almighty racket. At the start of every chorus, it is my solemn duty to bring

This time it's my turn to make an almighty racket

the two cymbals clashing together. I grin from ear to ear as my mum watches proudly from the front row. This noise brought me great delight.

A cacophony which didn't is one that I experienced when I lived with my first wife, Lynn, in a flat in West Hampstead. On the whole, our neighbours were very nice. Unfortunately, the lady downstairs (an actress) had rented out her flat to a member of a pop group riding the wave of the ecstasy culture.

Aside from the fact that said pop star had a predilection for playing music VERY loud, any time day or night, they also seemed to enjoy what sounded like very complicated mating rituals. (David Attenborough would've been interested in a recording of their pairing ceremonies, I'm sure.)

On one occasion at three in the morning I confronted him about the music, thrust a set of headphones into his hands and suggested he use them. It was an unwise decision. I never saw them again.

Noise annoys.

This morning, the first day of the new academic year, I rose at 7 a.m., opened the bedroom windows and looked out at the garden. Squirrels were playing. Wood pigeons were strutting about their business. A solitary woodpecker was tap-tap-tapping away on an apple tree. For a moment, all was calm. Tranquil even.

Then I heard something. It was a low drone. It grew louder over the next half-hour. No, it wasn't my stomach rumbling. It was the sound of the M25.

What the **world** needs now is . . . a great **big bucket** of *hush*

When the singer-songwriter Chris Rea described it as 'The Road To Hell', he wasn't wrong. For those of us who have to navigate it, we're often left breathless by the sheer stupidity of those who treat it like a racetrack. That is, of course, on the rare occasion the motorway hasn't ground to a standstill, when we're left passively inhaling the virulent vapours from the plonker in front, or bursting our blood vessels over the dipstick who obviously thinks his time is more important than ours as he tries to squeeze his Chelsea tractor into the tiniest space just in front of our tax disc.

Where did we all go wrong?

Well, I think it's inherent selfishness. Everyone is so bound up with themselves and their own agendas we've forgotten how to live. We've forgotten how to give.

What the world needs now is . . . a great big bucket of *hush*. We need time to reflect, time to breathe. Even time to pray.

And one day, when the benign dictator that lurks inside of me is given the supreme political platform, I will make it mandatory: shut up or be shot.

You know it make sense.

NICK'S NOTES THINGS TO DO

✔ SLOW DOWN WHENEVER I CAN

✔ SHUT UP SO OTHERS CAN TALK

✔ LISTEN BECAUSE I MIGHT LEARN SOMETHING

✔ WORK, REST AND PRAY

3

THE VELVET ROPE

It can still make the hackles rise on the back of my neck when I think about it.

'I'm sorry, sir. You can't come in here, you're not wearing a tie.'

And with that, I was ushered discreetly, but firmly, from a very upmarket restaurant. It was the kind of place that sized you up as you walked in, checking out jewellery and clothing – not to mention the car from which you emerged. I should've known not to go. But I just hated the 'them and us' attitude of places like that.

I still do.

Fast forward to a well-known, posh nightclub a few years later. Same principle applies. There is a velvet rope behind which sit the famous, the very nearly famous, and their coke-dealing buddies who always managed to wheedle their way in, doling out little 'bumps' as they went.

Now I didn't want to belong to that club. But I hated the fact that they thought they were better than we were. I'm firmly balanced with a chip on both shoulders – and any type of exclusion irks me.

I'm **firmly balanced** with a **both** chip on shoulders

I have to admit, I've been to churches that feel the same. They were cold, stiff-necked, unrelenting places with not so much a grin as a grimace as you walked in. But times and people change – thank God. And I'm grateful (what an understatement) that there is no velvet rope between me and my heavenly father. Though I might've been guilty of creating my own such barriers in the past through a wilful and misguided youth, today I know I belong.

It's that very sense of belonging – knowing you're in the right place and knowing you're forgiven – that I want to share with as many people as possible.

Jesus loved outsiders. Be they lepers, conmen or hookers. His was not – and is not – an exclusive club. It's open to everyone. And that, for me, is the challenge: to have the grace to include everyone. To welcome them genuinely into my home, into our church, and into our lives. And it costs. Sometimes we have to try and bury our selfish desires to bless others. But that's no bad thing. After all, the ultimate price was paid on the nail.

After all, the **ultimate price** was paid **on the nail**

NICK'S NOTES THINGS TO DO

✔ WELCOME THE STRANGER

✔ DON'T BE A SNOB

✔ TAKE AWAY THE VELVET ROPE

✔ FORGET MYSELF

4

ONE GIANT LEAP

It is the summer of '66. England are about to win the gleaming Jules Rimet Trophy and Geoff Hurst and Martin Peters are about to leave an indelible mark on the beautiful game of football. 'I bet you can't jump off that porch,' said my mate Andy.

'I can. You just watch!' I cried, leaping like a lemming into empty space. I hurtled to the ground, badly twisting my ankle and embedding my face in our front lawn.

I lay writing in agony on the ground

'Ouch! That really hurts!' – I lay writhing in agony on the ground.

From that day on, I've never been fond of heights. That applies whether it's looking over a cliff, going up a ladder or sitting in a flimsy metal membrane in the sky that man in his arrogance has decided to string together. I know the statistics. It's safer to fly than go by car, boat or train. But I just don't buy it.

There's something deeply disconcerting about being in a plane with 300 others while God boots the thing around like it was a football on the end of David Beckham's toe. And let's not forget even he, greatly gifted as he is, doesn't always put the ball in the back of the net (Beckham, that is).

I remember flying out to the Frankfurt Music Fair with eighties pop group Kajagoogoo. It was winter – and it had been more than a bumpy ride. In fact, it was more like a roller coaster. As we descended into Frankfurt, I could see the snow on the ground, and then about a hundred feet below us, a plane. At that precise moment our own craft veered sharply and began to shudder as the pilot tried to abort the landing. Every metal joint, bolt and frame seemed to jar and screech as we narrowly avoided joining old Volkswagens at the local knackers yard.

The cabin went silent. There were no announcements. There was hardly a heartbeat. Ten minutes later, the pilot – who by the way was German – piped up. 'I'm very sorry,' he said, like a character from the movie *Airplane*, 've have to make ze over-shoot, uzzervise ve hit ze uzzer plane.'

We didn't warm to such candour. When we finally made it down to the ground, there was a sardonic round of applause from the largely British passengers who had chosen to fly with the famous German airline. There was also a collective sigh – accompanied by the faint aroma of flatulence – as people sought to contain their relief.

Back in the sixties, flying was glamorous. Air hostesses were scions of beauty and politeness, and not treated with disdain as 'trolley dollies' by chauvinist males. The smartly dressed customs officer would proudly chalk an 'X' on your luggage as it was checked. It was exotic. Something that film stars did.

I remember flying to Jersey once – and the excitement that came with it. I even bought a metal model of the Vickers Viscount we flew on. Nowadays, you go through security where every last item of hand luggage is minutely examined or, worst case scenario, taken away from you. You dispose of any liquids that are viewed as suspicious, because as we all know, aftershave is the latest weapon of mass destruction. Woe betide you if you're foolish enough to complain. You're treated to an intimate body search that leaves your mouth dry with fear and your eyes watering. Without doubt, the worst place for this animal-like experience is John F. Kennedy airport in New York. My wife and I made the mistake of carrying a video camera as part of our hand luggage. They took us apart. They took swabs from the camera to test for explosives. They were as intimidating as an NYPD blue with a nightstick in his hand can be. Post 9/11, we understand the need for such measures. But I wonder . . . couldn't there be a better way of going about things?

One **giant leap** can get you into a lot of
trouble

Rock climbing is also hazardous for those of us with a fear of heights. That's what I discovered when I tried to climb up Stanage Edge in Derbyshire. Your body can freeze and muscles cramp. This normally takes place about halfway up. And the climb should never, ever be attempted with just a washing line. That I am here today to tell the tale is a testament to the level-headedness of my mates who helped me inch-by-inch up and over the craggy outcrop until I lay exhausted on the top.

One giant leap can get you into a lot of trouble. But sometimes we have to take a step of faith in order to grow. And from my own personal experience, that's normally a painful process – if ultimately worthwhile.

As I write, my first book is about to be published and I'm amazed. First, because I didn't know if I'd have the discipline to ever complete it. Second, because I never expected to find a publisher. Third, because the amount of time it took to write left me strapped for cash – as it took me away from my day job, working in the music business. It was one giant leap. As for me, I wait, prayerfully, only God knows the outcome.

The fishermen mending their nets by the shores of Lake Galilee also took a leap of faith. They met with Jesus, heard what he said, made what some might consider a rash decision, and chose to follow him.

Did it cost them? Yes, I believe it did.

Was it worth it? Yes, I believe it was.

And it costs us now even in the twenty-first century. I may not like heights, ladders and flying. I may not be Spiderman. But the places God takes me – sometimes physically, emotionally, mentally and spiritually – often involve extreme effort, sometimes sacrifice.

Yet if you find yourself climbing what you feel is an insurmountable mountain, and you just can't cope, reach out . . . and take God's hand. Remember when you finally get to the top, you'll see the most spectacular view.

And you know, I'd hate to miss that.

NICK'S NOTES THINGS TO DO

✔ TAKE A GOOD BOOK WHEN I GO ON A LONG
  FLIGHT

✔ REMEMBER THAT GOD IS WITH ME WHEN I
  TRAVEL

✔ PRAY FOR FRIENDS AND FAMILY WHO HAVE TO
  COMMUTE

✔ HAVE PATIENCE WITH AIRPORT OFFICIALS

✔ DON'T FORGET MY SENSE OF HUMOUR

5

THE BALANCING ACT

I sometimes feel like a juggler with too many balls in the air. At other times I feel like Jim Carrey's character Bruce in the movie *Bruce Almighty* watching the computer screen as all the prayers and demands flood in. Out of sheer frustration he replies, 'Yes to all.'

Often that's how I feel. But I'm more likely to reply in the negative across the board than the positive. And then I feel like a clown that's fallen off the circus pony the wrong way, one time too many.

I feel like a
clown
that's fallen off the
circus pony

As I work from home, from time to time the boundaries get blurred. All too often I'll be working on a piece of music or doing what I'm doing now, trying to come up with something that might be of interest and be thought-provoking (on a good day). Suddenly the door to my studio will burst open. Enter my wife wanting some advice on something, or one or both of my daughters wanting help with their homework, or to tell me about their day, or on occasion to complain about something.

Sometimes they all arrive at once – without fail usually when I'm in the middle of a tense phone conversation – all needing to express how they feel. At this point my dog Max will also start barking as the doorbell rings . . .

You see the secret of comedy is . . . timing. And I feel like I'm never fully prepared for what comes next. Yet it's vital we listen to one another. Just as it is vital to try and listen to God.

How do we make time to listen to him? And why do we choose almost anything to do or focus on – apart from our heavenly father?

Are we pre-conditioned to give him the glory on a Sunday, singing all the latest praise and worship songs, but the rest of the week give him the hump because we ignore him in favour of more pressing 'worldly' demands?

Now I know that we need to go out and earn the dosh to put food on the family table but how do we get the balance right, between serving God and looking after the immediate needs of our families and those we love?

Well, just like everything else in life, it's not easy. It's about as difficult as trying to locate Osama Bin Laden in Afghanistan or getting the Zimbabwean leader Robert Mugabe to admit that his greed and selfishness have ruined his country and his people.

It means we have to seek to put God first

OK, so it's not *that* difficult, but you get the picture. In which case, where should we start? Well I hate to say this, because my life is woefully unstructured and largely lacking in discipline, but I'm afraid I think that's what we need: some structure. We should try and build some kind of routine into our daily lives that allows time to breathe, think, watch, pray and listen.

And that means *deliberately choosing* to make the time. Just as in our house after getting up in the morning we deliberately choose to say a quick family prayer and see the kids safely off to school.

It means we have to seek to put God first. Forgetting is not an option.

NICK'S NOTES THINGS TO DO

✔ REMEMBER HOW BLESSED I AM TO HAVE A FAMILY

✔ TAKE SOME SMALL STEPS TO ADD STRUCTURE IN CERTAIN AREAS OF LIFE

6

LIFE IN THE FAST LANE

What is it about young men and cars? They pass their driving test. Then they pass us on the road hurtling everywhere at a million miles an hour endangering life and limb – not just to themselves but to the rest of us road users, too. It's as if they're in a hurry to get to heaven. They zoom around in mum's or dad's car while talking continually on their mobile phone, seemingly oblivious to anything else going on around them. It makes my blood boil.

The more serious offenders will have their own exclusive set of wheels, customised with a set of speakers and bass-boom-box that must be loosening most of the car's nuts and bolts as they speed along, usually late at night with everything – car, stereo and themselves – cranked to the max. Testosterone flowing freely, they let us know who is 'The Man'.

On occasions they're lippy and surly and will shout abuse as they cut you up in traffic, suggesting that one

On occasions they're **lippy and surly**

has *onanist* tendencies. If only they knew the deep irony of that particular remark.

How are we supposed to respond? Well, on a human level, I want to throttle them. On another, I think the response has to start at home. And I think the father should take greater responsibility in educating his son in the correct and courteous ways of conducting oneself on Her Majesty's highways.

The problem is, more and more children are growing up with absentee dads. As a result, we're reaping a harvest of angry young men.

So . . . what is the Christian response?

Well, it's difficult. We can only try to be better dads to our own kids. We can be loving and consistent husbands so our children feel secure in the family environment. And we can pray for patience and safety on a daily basis as we step into our own vehicles.

It's far from easy. Yet we do need to try and model some of the gifts our heavenly father gives us: grace, compassion, meekness.

And when all else fails, I always resort to this:

'GOD, HELP!'

He usually does. Unless that morning my soul is hard of hearing.

Life in the fast lane? Not for me, buddy. My God leads me beside still waters.

Life in the fast lane? Not for me, buddy

NICK'S NOTES THINGS TO DO

✔ TRY NOT TO GET CHEESED OFF WITH YOUNG MALE DRIVERS – I WAS A PLONKER ONCE MYSELF

✔ DON'T EVER USE A MOBILE WHEN DRIVING

✔ REMEMBER THAT BEING A DAD IS ONE OF THE MOST IMPORTANT THINGS I'LL EVER DO

7

RADIATING SOMEWHERE NEAR YOU

Ever wanted to glow in the dark? For some time I've felt a profound disquiet about appliances that give off radiation. You know the kind of things – microwaves, mobile phones, both in and outside the house – and probably this very laptop I'm vigorously typing away at.

I have friends in the armed forces who've been around military and naval hardware most of their lives. They claim there's little harm done. But it's not just the radio waves – it's what they carry – that worries me.

A young girl can be sitting on the train and receive something highly inappropriate via Bluetooth. But she may have no idea it was sent by someone sat opposite her who clearly doesn't have the best of intentions. Honourable or otherwise.

The content of what teenagers send – even on relatively safe platforms like MSN – is alarming. I've discovered that by hiding behind your computer screen or text messaging service, people and teenagers in particular will write things to each other they would

The content of what teenagers send is alarming

never *ever* dream of saying, face-to-face.

Gone are the days when your best mate might go up to the girl/boy you liked and say, 'My mate fancies you . . . will you go out with him/her?' Now there are seemingly a hundred different libidinous ways to communicate, often in far more graphic and detailed terms than you can possibly imagine (or frankly want to), about what you'd like to do to/with that person.

Innocence is being eroded, by absence of proper boundaries, by the information super-highway that will deliver anything to your computer you so desire. The effect this is having on our kids – from what their peer group is up to alone – is devastating.

You can't survive 30 years in the music business and be a prude. And I'm not one. But somehow we have to find a way of being there for our children as they navigate through these silicon swamplands, and electronic everglades. The terrain might look interesting to them, but beneath its surface lurk the human equivalent of snapping turtles and menacing alligators.

How do we help them? Well, to tell you the truth, I don't have the formula for an antidote. Not very helpful, is it? But I want to share these thoughts with you, if I may. Being there for them is vital. At least if we're around, we can be a sounding board or even a kicking post when they're unsure of what to do.

Try putting in some boundaries. After a couple of disappointing incidents, we decided mobiles are kept downstairs along with computers, and that any friends coming round can 'check' their mobile at the door and pick it up on their way out.

Now I know that might make me sound like a benign dictator but I've found it does help a little when it comes to policing stuff.

You might also like to think about a curfew for Internet activity. Then your child has time to wind down properly before going to bed, rather than get into an electronic frazzle.

And the final and most important thing is to pray. Pray often. Pray hard and call out to God for help and wisdom in all dealings with your children. We love them, but even the best-behaved child will exacerbate you from time to time. So pray for patience, too.

Be **kind** to yourself when you get **things wrong**

Be kind to yourself when you get things wrong – and be kind to them, too. We're all learning – some of us at a slower pace than others! Laughter round the meal table is really important. That's where a lot of our major ups-and-downs are sorted. It's so vital. That's where everyone has the opportunity to share what's been going on in their lives that day.

We may be surrounded by new technology radiating away but the best communication is to look someone in the eye and talk to them – while never forgetting to listen to what they have to say. We need to invest in that more.

Forget buying your son or daughter the latest mobile phone or laptop. Why not try and buy yourself some time with them? One to one. Face to face.

You know, we're constantly being told, 'The future's bright, the future's Orange.' Well, if we can just stick to our guns, and make time for each other, I'd suggest the future is an awful lot brighter than that.

NICK'S NOTES THINGS TO DO

✔ IF I MUST HAVE A PHONE, I MUST GET THE CHEAPEST, SAFEST AND SIMPLEST POSSIBLE

✔ I MUST PUT ALL ELECTRONIC HARDWARE UNDER CLOSE SURVEILLANCE

✔ I MUST LISTEN TO WHAT MY KIDS ARE SAYING

8

SPROUTS

What is the attraction of sprouts? They're foul-tasting, ugly-looking vegetables. And when consumed, they cause one to explode so much methane into the atmosphere that they can treble a lifetime's carbon emissions.

I could **understand** if they were **pretty**

I could understand if they were pretty. But their colour tends to look like an anaemic leprechaun.

Maybe my hatred of this rotund, testicular-like vegetable springs from my formative years. I have a painful memory of having to sit at the dining table with my lunch finished all bar the one lonely sprout, cold on my plate, as my mother and I engaged in a battle of wills over it.

'You can't have your pudding until you've eaten it.'

'I HATE it!' I would scream.

After sitting there in fury for half an hour, I would relent and stick the disgusting, bitter, very cold and smelly thing in my mouth.

My wife reliably informs me that they help improve alkalinity in our bodies. Apparently, that's very good for our western diet and particularly for . . . ahem . . . sperm. Sperm like sprouts? Hardly romantic.

Yet for those of us in need of filling one more pram, forget fossil fuels, Chelsea tractors and new airport terminals. It's time to eat your greens!

NICK'S NOTES THINGS TO DO

✔ REMEMBER THE FIVE-A-DAY RULE!

9

AMERICAN EXCESS

'Money, it's a gas. Grab that cash with both hands and make a stash.'
('Money', Roger Waters)

A profound mistrust of financial institutions has always been part of my portfolio. From an early age, I seemed to be besieged with credit cards and wonderful offers from our flexible friends. I was never much of a saver, more of a spender. Nobody ever taught me about money and how to be responsible with it.

So my credit rating for years resembled the score line of a Vauxhall Conference football club who'd endured a drubbing at the hands of the mighty Manchester United. In my twenties, I suspect I must have paid hundreds of pounds in interest on maxed-out credit cards. It took me a long time to learn how to manage my money.

Something about the lure of plastic and show business just seemed to bring out the worst in me. Whether it was fancy clothes, or expensive bottles of wine in rarefied restaurants, I was a sucker for all that lifestyle stuff. I had *American excess*.

I had American excess

It also didn't help that I was slow on the uptake. When I set up my first business while I was single, I didn't give it a second thought when the bank asked me to guarantee my overdraft. After all, it was all going to go swimmingly, wasn't it? Surely I was going to be *very* successful.

It turned out to be a lesson learned. A lesson learned the hard way. I struggled to pay off the bank's demands – while trying to keep my business afloat. Still, it was the eighties, and we were all enraptured with 'Yuppies' and 'Dinkies', cell phones the size of bricks *and* twice as heavy, and Thatcher's consumerist culture. Glossy-eyed and greedy, we seemed hell-bent on acquiring anything we thought we needed or might just need one day.

I watched an eighties pop group go through a million pounds in just over a year, no doubt believing they'd earn the same over the next 12 months. Then I watched them brought to the edge of bankruptcy by the bank that couldn't do enough while they were rolling in it. When it came to the crunch, the hammer was brought down on them very firmly.

So it might come as a surprise when I tell you about one financial institution that has actually done something incredibly helpful. In fact, it's the complete opposite of all my experience during my twenties and early thirties.

For years now I've had a Platinum American Express card (just for the record I want you to know that I *do* know how pretentious that sounds). Basically, you pay £300 per year for a few perks and an excellent travel service and back-up, should you need it.

I saw such **grinding poverty** on a daily basis

However, I saw something else when I worked at an orphanage in Uganda. I saw such grinding poverty on a daily basis, I felt challenged to do something about it. On receiving my Platinum card, I rang them up and explained I was no longer comfortable having it, and could they reimburse the £300 and cancel my card immediately. I held my breath, anticipating a bit of a tussle. But the gentleman at the end of the line listened very carefully.

'We have a card especially for people like you,' he said, 'it's called the Red Card.'

Pardon me? For a moment I had visions of the referee sending off David Beckham in the England/Argentina game. Was this the credit card company way of politely but firmly telling me where I could stick my Platinum?

'How it works is like this,' he continued. 'There's no charge for using the card, and for every £1 you spend, one per cent goes directly to AIDS charities in Africa to help combat the disease.'

Not only that. They agreed to reimburse the £300 – and cancelled my Platinum card without further ado. I was shell-shocked. I was satisfied.

After years of American excess, I've now found a way to 'express' myself financially. Although I still need to address other areas of my giving, I do feel good about this. I don't want to bury my 'talents' in the ground, be they money, ability, time or love. I want God to take it all and use it, in spite of me, to his glory – and I've found one small way to do that.

Go on. *Express* yourself.

NICK'S NOTES THINGS TO DO

✔ THINK OF CREATIVE WAYS TO START GIVING

✔ THINK OF CREATIVE WAYS TO STOP TAKING

✔ CELEBRATE WHAT GOD HAS GIVEN ME

✔ CELEBRATE WHAT GOD CAN DO THROUGH ME

10

JOY

I have a picture in my head from Ken Russell's magnificent film adaptation of the epic seventies rock musical *Tommy*. It is of Roger Daltrey, lead singer from The Who, cart wheeling down a sandy beach. At the same time, his big rock voice thunders across the soundtrack, 'I'm f-r-e-e'.

To this day, it remains the first image that comes to mind when I think of joy. It is unfettered, unchallenged and liberating.

Other images also spring to mind: flying into Chicago in the winter of '86, my first time in America, seeing the lights spread out over the windy city as Simple Minds played on my Walkman, 'Don't you forget about me'. A sense of excitement, of adventure, of the new.

The birth of my daughters, hearing them cry for the first time, life-changing, forever committing, always feeding, never forsaking these bundles of joy.

To this day, it remains the **first image** that comes to **mind** when I think of **joy**

The profoundly deep joy when I realised God was going to give me a second chance with a new wife, having wrestled with him over the one I had lost.

For me, these are all moments of, at times, a tangible joy. The Bible encourages us through difficult times by promising us joy in the future. But what if we want and need joy, right now? What if we are in a miserable state, where joy seems the farthest away it could possibly be from us?

I've walked down that gravel road. I decided to look up at the stars – and not down into the mud. I decided to listen to the birds singing in the trees – and not the dull, monotonous drone of the traffic of misery that idled away in my mind. I decided to examine God's colourful palette as I walked my dog in the mornings, looking at his creation that surrounded me.

Don't get me wrong. I didn't see all his gloriousness for some time. But by making the effort, I gradually began to find a way through. Eventually, it led me to see him in ways that, during the dark times, I could only imagine.

And that, for me, is real joy. Sometimes we have to work at it but please be encouraged. He is a God of great faithfulness and fullness of joy.

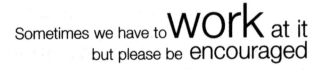

Sometimes we have to **work** at it but please be **encouraged**

NICK'S NOTES THINGS TO DO

✔ KEEP THE FIRE OF HOPE BURNING INSIDE

✔ WATCH OUT FOR THE 'HIDDEN' JOYS OF
EVERYDAY LIFE

✔ HELP OTHERS TO SPOT THE LIGHT IN THE
DARKNESS

11

MEN OF VIOLENCE

I've always thought that violence is the last resort of the inarticulate. As a former pugilist, I am aware of the physical pain dished out – having been on the receiving end of it (I had one very short painful fight . . . and lost).

I've always shied away from physical confrontation. In part, because I am not the tallest tree in the wood but also because I have an innate sense of self preservation. It just seems such a waste of time and so *very* painful.

> I've always shied away from physical confrontation

Yet from the dawn of time, man – and even nature – has seemed hell-bent on self-destruction. We've had countless 'holy wars' (what an oxymoron *that* is), barbaric crusades, people murdered and martyred for their beliefs. Sometimes we, the people, are as culpable as those who lead us by simply acquiescing rather than protesting against policies and decisions made by leaders and governments.

He is in
control

However, I think we have a choice. By choosing to be men and women of peace, it doesn't mean we have to be tigers in search of our dentures. We can lobby our politicians, our leaders and our God. We can petition all in prayer. We also can step out in our own small corner of this world, our home, our schools, our workplace.

Speak up. Speak out.

Not with any great 'Ta-dah!' But with a quiet, firm, resolute presence rooted in faith and belief that the God we serve is mighty to save. He is in control.

NICK'S NOTES THINGS TO DO

✔ LOBBY MY LOCAL MP ABOUT THE ISSUES THAT CONCERN ME

✔ WRITE TO THE NEWSPAPERS WHEN A STORY ENCOURAGES OR ALARMS US

✔ CONTACT TV CHANNELS WHEN THEY TRANSMIT SOMETHING THAT'S GOOD OR BAD

12

GLORIA IN ECCENTRICS

I was looking forward to being a recalcitrant 70-year-old full of peculiarities, petty little quirks and pedantic eccentricities. What fun! Then my wife lovingly informed me, in the wry way that she has, that I already possess those characteristics. If only there was something to look forward to . . .

> Joking apart,
> **I actually like**
> eccentrics

Joking apart, I actually like eccentrics. They make this world more colourful. And God frequently uses a maverick personality to do his work. John the Baptist was viewed to be a little 'touched' when he went about proclaiming there was going to be a Messiah who would change the world. That is, until the day when Jesus introduced himself.

And what kind of nutter would take on a giant like Goliath, armed only with a rudimentary catapult? Yet God triumphed through David and Goliath was defeated.

So is it the same today? I think the answer is, yes. I think that for some of us, God is asking us to say and do things which in earthly terms just don't make sense. We're being challenged to step out of our comfort zones and dance in the dragon's jaws.

For me, at this point in time, I'm being taught about patience and trust. I'm being taught how to get the balance right between striving in my own strength and waiting and resting in God. And at times it is very hard. I lost control when I lost my first wife to cancer and am still struggling in my day-to-day life not to hold on to people or things, but to be able to surrender them to God.

You know the hymn, 'All to Jesus I Surrender'? I'm pretty sure if most people were honest, they would admit they have a mental checklist of things they can't or aren't quite ready to give up (which they do their level best to hide from God).

What a waste! Imagine the freedom in Christ we'd really have, if instead of making a largely rhetorical statement, we actually tried to live like that on a daily basis. The world would be changed.

And if by chance God asks me to do something **outrageous,** I won't be surprised!

So with today's rant over, I'm going to quietly try to surrender everything to Jesus every day. And you know, I feel like a toddler all over again – I'm learning to walk. If I fall down flat on my backside, I'm sure I'll hear a still, small voice urging me to get up and try again. And if by chance God asks me to do something outrageous, I won't be surprised!

NICK'S NOTES THINGS TO DO

✔ WHAT CAN I GIVE UP TODAY, THAT HINDERS MY FAITH?

✔ WHERE CAN I GO TO FIND SOME TIME AND SPACE TO GET WITH GOD?

✔ HOW CAN I START TO SURRENDER TO JESUS ALL THE THINGS I KEEP HOLDING BACK?

13

HUNGER

In the early eighties, I always joked that I 'starved for a living'. The reality was that I couldn't bring myself to sign on. In my skinny, arrogant state, I perceived that as a failure.

So largely I lived on a diet of cornflakes and water

So largely I lived on a diet of cornflakes and water, coupled with the pots of taramasalata and pitta bread that my friend Rachel used to give me and on occasions, as a treat, a McDonald's. They hadn't invented the 'Happy Meal' then. I wasn't able to fully appreciate the delicious irony.

Since then, the near skeletal frame has gone. In its place is much greater largesse. But the hunger has not. It's just different. If you've ever honestly not known where your next meal is coming from, it does funny things to you.

I might've been poor, yes. But I had a roof over my head. And back then there were no other mouths to feed, just my own. I didn't, and still don't, live in a hut with a corrugated iron roof that leaks; have a stick to hang my belongings on; use a hole in the ground as my latrine; have to care for four children who are desperate to be fed and clothed. Yes, some people do live like that. I had the privilege of meeting them. They were generous to a fault.

What am I hungry for, then? Selfishly . . . that both my children walk with God and know his loving nature. That they would 'walk humbly, love mercy, and act justly' – as the prophet Micah said. That we might be able to add to our family. That I may, by God's grace, be able to provide for us all. That I would be a better husband and father. But nobody's dying here. So what should be my response to those who are? Well, I'm not going to say it's up to the individual. It's not. That'd be the easy way out.

What did Jesus say?

> 'For I was hungry, and you fed me. I was thirsty, and you gave me a drink. I was a stranger, and you invited me into your home. I was naked, and you gave me clothing. I was sick, and you cared for me. I was in prison, and you visited me.'
> (Matthew 25:35,36)

Whether we have a **little or a lot,** there's always **more** we can do

And that's our challenge. Whether we have a little or a lot, there's always more we can do. While the poor are with us – spiritually, emotionally, financially – we must respond.

NICK'S NOTES THINGS TO DO

✔ WATCH WHAT I EAT

✔ WATCH WHAT OTHERS EAT

✔ DO SOMETHING ABOUT BOTH

14

I DON'T LIKE MONDAYS

Back in the days when I used to work for a living, I looked forward to Monday mornings. It was a chance to focus on the week ahead. Now in my current predicament of sporadic employment, I've come to dread them.

You see,
I'm 50 and still
want to work

You see, I'm 50 and still want to work. Yet the very industry I've inhabited for the last 30 years started calling me a veteran 10 years ago. I'm no longer fashionable or cutting edge, thin or handsome. Hopefully, my youthful arrogance has been replaced with both greater knowledge and wisdom and – maybe on a good day – even a little meekness.

From time to time, I potter into town to have lunch with my show business mates (those still in gainful employment). For the rest of my time, I'm trying to figure out just how I'll earn a living for the next 20 years.

Now if I'd been in the armed forces for the same period, I'd be retiring on a good pension with the possibility (after pulling a few strings) of a nice little second career. Perhaps as a non-executive director of a multinational company, or as a bursar at a college in Durham.

But no. I chose the haphazard route of the music business with no fixed income – and the possibility of perhaps writing or producing a worldwide hit with which to secure my future. I may have introduced the Spice Girls to my employers at the time, but had I written, produced or had a share in the publishing company I worked for, I would've been – as they put it in the early nineties – 'sorted'.

So I'll tell you **why** I don't like Mondays

So I'll tell you why I don't like Mondays. It's because I can, on occasions, feel a bit useless. Redundant, if you like. The girls go off to school. The rest of the world goes off to work. And I'm here writing to you. As the song says, 'What's it all about, Alfie?'

Well, as you see, I'm still trying to work it out. I know the glass is not so much half full as brim-full of possibilities. Yet my human condition feels like somebody's spilt my pint.

What can I do? Well, I'll go to lunch today to meet with my friend who owns a record label. I'll chat, smile – no doubt share my faith – and then come home. I'll leave no stone unturned looking for work. But at the end of the day, when I've exhausted all human possibilities, I'll try *very* hard to rest in God. To seek his presence. To try and unravel what *he* really wants me to do with the time left.

You see, I don't know. I can't see into the future. And God doesn't always make it obvious. But it's all about trust and obedience.

For me, it's quarter to nine on a Monday morning and time to get on my knees and pray. What else can I do?

NICK'S NOTES THINGS TO DO

✔ DO SOMETHING DIFFERENT ON A MONDAY

✔ PRAY SOMETHING DIFFERENT ON A MONDAY

✔ THANK GOD FOR TUESDAY!

15

BELIEF

It's wonderful when someone believes in you, wants the best for you, encourages you. It's such a gift to be given – and to be received. The knowledge that you are held in high esteem, respected – loved even – is a deep and full experience. 'To be held in the heart of a friend is to be a King,' is how Canadian singer-songwriter Bruce Cockburn put it.

It's **wonderful** when **someone** **believes** in you

What a glorious treasure to be so adored! Yet so it is with our heavenly father. He holds us in high esteem because he gave us his only Son, Jesus, so that we might rise up to be with him when our earthly days are done. But while we're here, we can invest in each other by believing and encouraging one another through the walk of life.

Back when I was a messed-up teenager, my parents believed I had a gift for the violin. So they paid for lessons and bought me a wonderful fiddle. If they hadn't, who knows where I might be – or how I would've turned out. As it was, they started me on a musical road that's lasted, rather scarily, for more than three decades now.

Chris Eaton has written countless songs for artists like Janet Jackson, Amy Grant, Vince Gill – and, for Sir Cliff Richard, composed the number one record 'Saviour's Day'. Chris told me his parents didn't mind what time of day he played the piano. They were just delighted that he'd found a way to be happy and express his talent. His parents believed in him. And the world would be a poorer place without his music.

Just as our Father God believes in us, so we have the chance to believe in each other. In our wives, husbands, children, relatives and friendships. And in so doing, we lift each other up, affirm, nurture and encourage each other.

I'm reminded of what Peter Coe used to do for his son Sebastian, when we were at school together. Most nights, once his homework was done, Seb would run. Most nights, his father would follow along in the car. It's all about belief.

We had a geography teacher at school who also spotted Seb's talent. I think his name was Mr Jackson. He arranged for a coach load of us to go and support Seb as he ran the cross country. He believed in him at least a decade before he won a gold medal at the Olympics. And his belief inspired us to believe, too.

It ended on a cross, with a father's tears

It started in a Bethlehem street, with a mother's smile. It ended on a cross, with a father's tears. It's all about belief.

NICK'S NOTES THINGS TO DO

✔ BELIEVE

✔ BELIEVE

✔ BELIEVE

✔ . . . AND BELIEVE AGAIN

16

LITTLE BITS OF PAPER

Our lives are like an untidy street, strewn with bits of paper. We sign away our rights the minute we open a current account, buy a car on credit or agree via the Internet to the manufacturer's terms and conditions. We employ lawyers to protect us when we buy a house, or sign a business contract. We're constantly putting our faith in man's wit and wisdom. What folly!

Hardly any of us **bother to** read the small print

Hardly any of us bother to read the small print, to check for the details discreetly tucked away. The whole system is set up to take advantage of you and me.

Just over a year ago we bought a PC laptop from a well-known manufacturer. The machine malfunctioned four times in the first year. It broke down again recently – just after the guarantee ran out. The manufacturer refused to do anything. In fact, they were incredibly rude to my wife when she sought redress. The retail chain we bought it from wrote to us and said they'd look into it. We felt like we were left high and dry.

And so it was I came home last week from a men's conference feeling peaceful, yet excited. I found my wife with steam coming out of her ears, as she recounted the day's events – and the injustice of it all. Apparently, as we'd bought the laptop through my company, in the wee small print there was a clause just for us. It basically said we had no rights at all.

The manufacturer had let us down. The service centre who'd repaired our computer a total of four times washed their hands of the whole affair. The jury was out on the retailer's conclusion.

My wife wasn't happy at all. Me? I was resolute in my infinite male wisdom. 'Sweetheart,' I stated blithely, 'our God is a great big God, and he says, "Vengeance is mine". If he wants to remedy the situation, he will – by finding someone in the organisation to turn it all around. He has the power.'

How easily that tripped off my tongue.

The next evening I walked in through the door. This time, my wife was beaming from ear to ear. 'Guess what?' she asked. 'The lady at the store said they didn't have to give us a new computer but they felt we'd been treated badly by the manufacturer and their repairs company. So in the interest of customer relations they'll let us replace the computer with one of the same cost. We have to go in and they'll ring the lady up and she'll authorise the return.'

It's been a lesson in justice and stewardship. We have such a consumer mentality here in the West, that the minute anything goes wrong we immediately seek to replace it. Some people even take this as far in their marriages, seeking a younger, faster model when the old one, reliable though it may be, shows signs of wear and tear. But what they really need is some TLC and a 100,000-mile service!

It would've been easy to walk away grumbling and muttering – which if I'm honest is probably what I would've done but my wife chose to think differently.

We're not called on to always quietly acquiesce

We're not called on to always quietly acquiesce, act like doormats or refuse bins for other people's gunk. Sometimes it's right, proper and good to take a stand.

And so God the author and creator of all things chose to bless my wife's quiet persistence and strong sense of justice. For which we give him the glory.

NICK'S NOTES THINGS TO DO

✔ CHECK THE SMALL PRINT WITH A BIG MAGNIFYING GLASS!

✔ CHECK THE STAR RATING ON SUPPLIERS VIA WEBSITES LIKE AMAZON

✔ CHECK OUT OF THIS CONSUMERIST SUB-CULTURE THAT CRIPPLES US ALL

17

HIGH FIDELITY

I was on a roll. One of our 'finds' – The Spice Girls – had become a global phenomenon. Our little publishing company enjoyed 44 UK Top 40 hits in just one year. I was frequently travelling to the States. It was the nineties and it was great.

It was the nineties and it was great

It was on one of those trips that I found my faith – and fidelity – tested. I was staying at The Malmaison opposite The Beverly Center in Los Angeles. I'd been out for dinner with some colleagues and a very attractive female pop star of the time. She was in 'LA' for a few days. After dinner, everyone came back to my suite. We chatted and drank some more, regaling each other with showbiz tales. Then it was time for everyone to leave.

How shall I put this? Well, let's just say I felt one of the party wanted to 'toy' with my affections.

Another time, I was in New York staying at The Ritz, Central Park (sorry, I'm honestly not trying to show off, just giving you some context!). I had a very enjoyable dinner with a female colleague. At the end of the evening, she wanted to linger longer than appropriate.

I'd be lying to you if I said I didn't find these women attractive. Maybe I was guilty of being woefully naïve.

I loved my wife. But because of her illness and all we were going through, (none of which was her fault), at times, I felt dreadfully lonely. Oh yes, I was successful in the world's eyes. So what? And I do believe it's possible to feel a sense of deep crushing despair and loneliness in a marriage. But for the record, absolutely nothing happened on both occasions.

> Oh yes, I was **successful** in the world's eyes. So what?

We take the vows of marriage on our wedding day. We mean them wholeheartedly. We discover their true implications as life unfolds.

Coming from a broken home and knowing the pain of infidelity and break-up, I could never break those vows, or the heart of my first wife or the hearts of my dear daughters. I've seen what happens when the vow breaks. It's not pretty. But as you've read, I'm not a saint. I'm in need of authority and accountability. Sometimes when we taste the sweet success the world has to offer we can become lost. And success is an aphrodisiac. Doors that had remained closed to you, suddenly spring open. People who wouldn't have looked twice at you before, suddenly start paying you more attention. That's the time we're at our most vulnerable. That's the time to cling to God and his Word – and not spiral out of control. I hate to say this, because I'm useless at it, but we need to be disciplined in carving out more time for God. When we're busy, we lose focus. Then things can start to go wrong.

Stay as close as you can to the highest power we know. Be smart. Don't put yourself in harm's way. If you're ambushed, get out quick! Run into the arms of your Saviour, who paid the highest price for our freedom.

Doing the stuff is not easy. The more you step out and grow in faith, you shouldn't be surprised when temptation is put in your way. But resist the devil, and he will leg it.

NICK'S NOTES THINGS TO DO

✔ TUNE IN TO HIGH FIDELITY

✔ DON'T LINGER WHEN LUST IS LURKING

✔ BE ACCOUNTABLE

18

LUMPS OF CLAY

Let's talk about vices. Everyone has a little, or not so little, safety valve for letting off steam. Some smoke, drink, shop, over-eat, over-exercise, over-control. How do you cope if you have the 'excess gene'?

And the more we **succumb** to the 'excess gene', the more **excuses** we create to **justify** our behaviour

Once I open a bottle of wine, I find it impossible not to finish it. I need greater self-control. Oh yes, I can argue my condition is partly due to the learned behaviour as a child growing up around an alcoholic – and at times the tragedy I've experienced. But we can all make excuses. And the more we succumb to the 'excess gene', the more excuses we create to justify our behaviour.

As a young man, one of my flatmates would max out their credit cards in a 'shop-till-you-drop' frenzy on a regular basis. Why did she do this? I think there were areas of her life she was deeply unhappy about. Despite her Christian faith, she still had a 'hole' in her heart.

I have another mate – now happy and healthy for nearly two decades – who used to ingest cocaine like you and I drink water. He came to regard it as an 'essential prerequisite'. It nearly killed him. Today, lots of young women seek to control the food they eat. Worried to the edge of paranoia by false and damaging media messages and peer group pressures, they become bulimic or anorexic putting their young lives at risk. Some self-harm as a way of controlling their pain.

I suspect it's about **owning up** and being totally **honest** with God

How do we build discipline and obedience into our lives, when some of our genetic foundations are so shaky?

The truthful answer: it's hard. I'm sure there are plenty of people out there who can provide glib textbook responses, some of which will be theologically justified. But for the ordinary man and woman, boy and girl, quietly, or maybe not so quietly, struggling . . . how do we cope?

I suspect it's about owning up and being totally honest with God. As Christians we're not supposed to have holes in our lives. It's all meant to be sorted and redeemed. But many of us do have them. We're works in progress: lumps of clay that have dried out a bit and need a little water before the potter reshapes us.

The first step is owning up. The second is to share the problem with someone. You're not alone. You'll probably find they're struggling with something as well – and you can encourage each other. Try and build in structure. When tempted to fall off your particular wagon, you can do something else to recapture your heart and imagination.

And pray. Prayer is a powerful weapon. God hears our cry from the deepest, darkest place. He does – and will – rescue you.

Finally, if you do fall off the wagon and feel wretched and useless, pick yourself up and climb back on again. There are millions of us just like you, lumps of clay in need of water and one more touch from the King.

NICK'S NOTES THINGS TO DO

✔ MONITOR MY INTAKE

✔ MONITOR MY OUTTAKE

✔ MAKE SURE I'M GIVING OUT MORE THAN TAKING IN

19

THE FAMILY OF DOG

For some 10 years, I've had a little canine friend in my life called Max. He's a miniature schnauzer. He has been, and remains, a wonderful companion. He has seen and witnessed things which, if he could talk, would make the hairs on the back of your neck stand on end. I love him to bits. Fortunately, he's very discreet.

He is also the only other alpha male in the house. Well, he was until recently. After 9 years, his all too frequent wanderlust finally caught up with him and he was hauled off to the vet for a little nip and tuck.

Ah yes it's a dog's life

On occasion, when I'm feeling sprightly, I vault out of bed in the morning and take Max for a walk by the River Chess. He's a wonderfully sociable dog with no preconceptions about other breeds or sexual orientation: he will wander off and talk to anybody. In the past, before his nip and tuck, he would seek to consummate the relationship in the only way he saw fit.

Ah yes it's a dog's life. But perhaps we can learn from our four legged friends. They're not terribly exclusive, and on the whole are warm and welcoming – although I wouldn't advocate giving visitors to your church a good lick while simultaneously jumping up and down, at least not the first time they step through the door! But there's a warmth and honesty – even transparency – to Max. He doesn't really need to talk. If he wants to pee, he'll stand by the back door. When he wants to come in, he'll bark once. If you're foolish enough to leave any food lying around that's accessible to a dog of his small stature, he will *always* eat it.

he'll go hurtling up the lawn to try and catch the interloper

He has no real agenda. He likes attention, to be fed and to be walked. The only time he gets barking mad is if he sees a squirrel or cat in our back garden. At that point his protective male hunter/gatherer instincts will kick in, and he'll go hurtling up the lawn to try and catch the interloper. But he never does. You see, Max may now be 10 years old, a little grey around the gills and our little nut-less wonder. But he really loves the family of dog.

NICK'S NOTES THINGS TO DO

✔ REMEMBER TO KEEP WALKING THE DOG

20

BEAUTY

It's 1980 and the heady days of the 'New Romantic' movement. I'm working with dance/mime group Shock, at London's Embassy Club. Suddenly, there's a commotion and lots of flapping around by the band's agents. An ice-cool vision with blonde hair and piercing blue eyes walks in and sits down quietly.

'Get her a drink – quick!' I hear the camper of the two agents say. 'She wants a glass of Perrier.'

I seize my opportunity before anyone else does, and take the beverage over to . . . Britt Ekland.

'Thank you,' she says. I don't quite know where to look. I am smitten. Yet somehow I manage to respond.

Beauty made me bashful

'You're welcome,' I say, before quickly turning away.

Beauty made me bashful.

Fast forward to the early nineties. I'm at a music festival in Germany called *Popkomm*. From the corner of my eye, I see a woman literally appearing to glide as she gracefully enters the room.

Every man and woman stops and stares.

A supermodel has just arrived to promote her record. She's just like a swan. Cool and elegant, aware of every eye in the room, she's a vision in ebony.

Sometimes the aroma is strong and heady

Then there's the type of beauty that can turn *anyone* into a bright shining star. You can see a different light in their eyes, a spring in their step, a radiance on their face. You hear a voice that's gentle and a laugh that's free and light, and so unique, it reminds you of a pebble skipping gently over the waves before sinking quietly from view. This person – whoever he or she is – clearly possesses something expensive and precious. There's a different kind of perfume in the air when they're around.

Sometimes the aroma is strong and heady. At other times it's more subtle and perhaps even fleeting. But over time you get to recognise it and also come to love it and the people who wear it. Not so much Lacoste but *the* cost.

It is the fragrance of Jesus.

NICK'S NOTES THINGS TO DO

✔ SPRINKLE THE SCENT OF JESUS OVER EVERYTHING I DO

✔ BREATHE IT IN

✔ BREATHE IT OUT

21

HEROES

Whenever I've met some of my favourite musicians, it's nearly always been disappointing. In the early eighties, I was introduced to one of Motown's legendary soul singers. High as a kite, he said, 'Nice to meet you. Could you excuse me while I go and powder my nose?' The boy from the white stuff.

There was the wonderful singer/songwriter from the north, whose work I admired greatly. He turned out to be one of the most dour and cynical people I've ever worked with. Bitter from a broken marriage, he was virtually bankrupt emotionally. If you looked in the dictionary under the word 'jaded' he would've probably typed his own name.

> # Bitter from a broken marriage, he was virtually bankrupt emotionally

Why is it part of the human condition that we admire people so much that we place them on pedestals? Then they fall off later of their own volition – or we knock them off when we think they're too big for their boots. Is this disease fundamentally British, or is it a pandemic across the globe?

Then there are people, often not extremely talented, who'll take the tiniest amount of integrity they can find and bury it as they strive to become a celebrity. It might be this week's household name fresh from the set of a reality TV show, a hero for 5 minutes coming to a tabloid near you (if you're not careful).

So who are the real heroes? History is littered with them – William Wilberforce, Lord Shaftesbury, Martin Luther King, Nelson Mandela, Dietrich Bonhoeffer. All have the same common denominator: they put the needs of others first. And they did so often at the expense of their own well-being. In some cases they paid the ultimate price with their lives.

I believe there are heroes all around us in everyday life. The neighbour who looks in on the elderly widow every day to make sure she's alright. The nurse in a hospital dispensing love and care to the sick, while clearing away the detritus that goes with all of that – underpaid and undervalued. A policeman risking his life to free a hostage, who doesn't have time to put on his bullet-proof vest before he has to kick down the door in order to save their life and risk his own. The wife caring for her terminally ill husband.

My Nana was my hero. She'd do anything to help anybody

Sometimes being a hero is putting ourselves in harm's way. It can also mean a quiet act of service. My Nana was my hero. She'd do anything to help anybody. She knew what life cost and what really mattered. It's a lesson to learn as we count down the days to eternity.

NICK'S NOTES THINGS TO DO

✔ ANONYMITY IS A GOOD THING

✔ FAME IS FLEETING AND FATUOUS

✔ JESUS IS MY HERO

22

THE CHUCKLE MUSCLE

'The happiest people the world has ever known have always been those who have had the glorious view of salvation . . . and so they live as more than conquerors in this world and are immune to most of the things that are finally responsible for all our unhappiness and miseries.'

(Dr Martyn Lloyd-Jones)

I love the sound of laughter

I love the sound of laughter. Be it my own or other people's, it's such a liberating sound. There's something totally releasing about giggling uncontrollably – particularly in groups.

I laugh a lot. I even laugh a lot in church. And I've learned to recognise my fellow minstrels of mirth. They have a light in their eyes and a spring in their step that comes from the divine. It's wonderful to be around them. If only I could be like that all the time.

I like old-fashioned comedians. I'm forever watching re-runs of Jimmy Tarbuck and the late but incredibly quick-witted Bob Monkhouse – masters of mirth and the one-liner. The not-so-new breed like Paul Merton are wonderfully agile, and think on their feet in a way that I find breathtaking. In fact, I can't think of anything better than laughing till I burst. OK, maybe one thing.

Will there be laughter in heaven? Well, I believe there will be a great deal of joy. In fact, since I hit 50 I've been thinking a lot more about eternity than before. Will it be comfortable? Will there still be the wonder of a DFS sofa sale? Will there be any politics left? Or will the angels have a three-line whip to bring everyone into compliance?

And when I meet God, what will he say? Can you imagine the

dialogue, 'Well now, it was a game of two halves. You certainly lost the first. And if it hadn't been for my Son coming off the subs bench in extra time, you'd have lost the second as well!'

I can see myself – tears rolling down my face, tongue-tied at the enormous grace of it all. My Jesus, my Saviour, coming to my rescue.

Will I be exercising my chuckle-muscle? Yes, I think so. I have this wonderful picture of thousands of people lying on their backs like tortoises, waving their legs in the air weeping tears of joy and gratitude, literally laughing their socks off.

The comedic cacophony of the extremely thankful.

NICK'S NOTES THINGS TO DO

✔ HELP THE CHURCH TO LAUGH

✔ HELP THE WORLD TO LAUGH

✔ REMEMBER TO LAUGH AS MUCH AS POSSIBLE

23

HEALTH AND FITNESS

My publisher (God bless him) is an incredibly fit man who runs marathons on a regular basis. He is lithe and trim – despite his advancing years – a born athlete.

In my twenties, I was **handsome and thin** on the **outside,** but my **mind** and **soul** were in **terrible** shape

I, on the other hand, resemble a large Chesterfield sofa. Deeply comfortable and familiar, but just a little too big for your lounge. Not so much a body politic as body rhetoric. I say all the right things – yet I'm at a loss when it comes to doing them.

What is health and fitness? In my twenties, I was handsome and thin on the outside, but my mind and soul were in terrible shape. Now I like to think on occasion that I'm sorted in the mind and soul department – even if the physical side isn't necessarily what it should be. But what can I say? I think denial is a river in Egypt.

My wife and children urge me to live a healthier lifestyle. I know I must one day, but I keep putting it off. Why? Well, I suppose I associate it with saying 'goodbye' to a lot of the finer things in life. Fine wine and gorgeous slabs of Chaume, Camembert and Brie that just run off my plate and into my stomach. I do feel that perhaps I treat my earthly body with not enough due care and attention. But it's the balance between putting years into your life or life into your years.

Time to face up to responsibilities and take the plunge

Having said that, the thought of waking up on a hospital gurney wired up to all sorts of weird and wonderful machines is definitely *not* appealing. I already take statins for high cholesterol and sleep with a mask over my face that pumps air into my lungs to stop the airways from collapsing. Perhaps in writing this I'm prescribing what must happen – and soon.

Time for change. Time to face up to responsibilities and take the plunge.

Time to walk the dog.

NICK'S NOTES THINGS TO DO

✔ EAT LESS

✔ EXERCISE MORE

✔ WALK TO THE CHEESE SHOP

24

FATHERHOOD

I'm going to be a dad again. And for the most part, I'm absolutely delighted about it. However, I'm now 50. That means I feel a little like Abraham. On an earthly level, I'm worried witless about how I'll provide for him/her (working title, by the way, is 'Tiger') for the next 20 years or so.

Yet from a spiritual perspective, I know that after 27 months of trying, this baby is a living example of God's miraculous grace. So if I can trust him for our unborn child, I should be able to relax about his provision for us. And yet if I'm honest, I'm struggling.

You need your **dinner** on the table at . **six**

You see, it's the balance between going out – and literally at times foraging – for work, then resting in the knowledge that *Jehovah Jireh* (God our provider) has it all under control. That's hard. The northern male in me, the 'If ever tha does owt for nowt do it for thee sen', is still latent and needs exorcising. You know the maxim. It's Friday night. You come home from work. You need your dinner on the table at six, off down the pub for a few pints at seven and if the missus is feeling like it, nooky after closing time!

Believe it or not, as a young man that was what I imagined marriage would be like. It's only thanks to the endless patience of womankind that I can honestly say that I've moved on from such patently prehistoric values. But being a dad again just blows my mind.

First time around 15 years ago, I thought Misha, my daughter, was a porcelain doll. Even with her sister Jodie – born 19 months later – we treated her very carefully. I think being a dad to two teenage girls is a massive privilege but not without its pressures. I struggle with my control freakery as they grow up. I also feel it's not as nice a world out there as it used to be. They're also very beautiful – and young men have recently started to show more than a passing interest.

I feel like buying a big ferocious dog – and acquiring a shotgun licence – to keep the pesky little varmints at bay!

If our new baby is a boy I'm going to buy him a baby-sized Manchester United football kit. And if it's a girl? The same.

If I'm struggling now, how will it be in 15 years' time when I'm 65?! I think the answer will be . . . a lot of fun. Challenging, life-enhancing, thought-provoking and wonderfully rewarding. Though I can never replace what little hair I'll have lost in the process, life is for living. Let's seize the day.

Though I can never replace what little hair I'll have lost in the process life is for living. Let's seize the day

NICK'S NOTES THINGS TO DO

✔ SOME PRE-BIRTH VISITS TO MOTHERCARE COULD HELP TO GET BACK INTO PARENTING

✔ VISITING BOYS MUST SHOW PASSPORTS AT THE FRONT DOOR

✔ IF A SHOTGUN ISN'T BIBLICAL, HOW ABOUT AN ANCIENT ISRAELITE SWORD?

25

THE SEPTEMBER OF MY YEARS

OK, I'll own up. I've started frequenting charity shops in search of vinyl treasure. Today, one of the lilies in the dustbin I found was a simply gorgeous Frank Sinatra album, titled, *The September of My Years*. It resonated with me, as I've just completed my half-century. I can see the view from the hill.

Frankly, I'm amazed to have made it, having taken so many wrong turns along the way

Frankly, I'm amazed to have made it, having taken so many wrong turns along the way. Like Frank, I did it 'My Way' for quite a few years, but I always felt I was like a piece of elastic. At times I'd stretch far away from God but at the critical moment I'd come 'pinging' back to the God of 'second chances'. I've lost count of how many he's given me, but I remember the significant ones. Imagine the limitless patience he must have with each of us.

I feel good about life in the September of my years. I do worry about being a dad again and the implications of that as I get older. And as the self-styled hunter-gatherer, protector-provider, I have to hand all of that to God every single day as soon as I wake up in the morning – or be overwhelmed by it. It's all taken on trust.

What about the times I've trusted God for things and it hasn't worked out the way I thought? What about the countless nights I begged him to spare my first wife Lynn's life? He didn't answer that the way I expected. So it can be hard to trust God when things don't work out the way we plan.

I'm simply choosing to believe God knows what's best for me

At some point you may have felt disappointed by God – or even let down. But is it him or us? Is it our lack of faith, or the simple fact that we cannot presume to understand the mind of God? I've lain alone at night pondering that one many times. I've come to this reluctant conclusion: we won't know until we get to the ultimate *Question Time* in heaven.

So what about the next 50 years? I'm simply choosing to believe God knows what's best for me. Don't get me wrong, I'm not abdicating responsibility. But what is faith unless we can trust? I'm here, aren't I? Did I have a hand in my creation? No. Do I know when I'm going to shuffle off this mortal coil? No. Do I know where I'm going? Yes.

Do you?

NICK'S NOTES THINGS TO DO

✔ TRUST IS A CHOICE. CHOOSE TRUST.

✔ PRAY FOR THE CONFIDENCE TO TRUST

26

IS YOUTH WASTED ON THE YOUNG?

I sometimes wish I'd had the knowledge and (hopefully) wisdom I have now, when I was much younger. I think Rod Stewart may have even written a song along those lines. But would life have turned out any different?

> Hindsight is 20/20 vision, clear as a bell

Hindsight is 20/20 vision, clear as a bell. But in order to grow, don't we have to make some mistakes along the way – to learn a little about life?

I think we do. It can be a painful process, though. And as you get older, I think the recovery process can take longer. So why do some of us fly and others crash and burn? A large part of the answer can be as a result of our childhood, maybe hurts collected along the way that we haven't been able to work through or get help for. But I also think it's about choice.

For example, when something has deeply upset us, for how long do we hold on to that anger? Like a child with a cut that's just healing, do we keep picking at the scab until it bleeds again?

Let's carry the metaphor further. The wound may have been cleaned and the antiseptic and plaster applied. Do we then move on with our lives until the pain that was so excruciating becomes a gentle throb and then disappears, leaving a faint scar on our body, mind or soul?

> Some people seem to have a **personality** that **bounces back** from anything

Some people seem to have a personality that bounces back from anything. For others it can take longer to get over hurts. Yet many of us become adept at hiding what's eating at us. Sometimes the hurt recurs as emotional indigestion years later.

What does the Bible say? Well, the apostle John had a vision of what's possible. In the book of Revelation, he wrote a sweet promise for any of us who feel we've been wounded by life, or are still carrying pain that we need to jettison: 'He will wipe every tear from their eyes, and there will be no more death or sorrow or crying or pain.' (Revelation 21:4).

Come and do it, Lord. Amen.

NICK'S NOTES THINGS TO DO

✔ REMEMBER TO FORGET (ABOUT HURTS)

✔ REMEMBER THAT OUR GOD IS THE GOD OF ALL COMFORT

27

PERSONAL SPACE

I'm not very good at sharing. I think, or like to persuade myself, that it's because I grew up as an only child but the truth is probably a lot starker than that. I'm selfish. Don't get me wrong. I love being married, being a dad and all that. But some things I really struggle with.

But some things I really **struggle** with

I was in Nashville last year. One thing that struck me was how much land people had around their homes. Even in the not-so-well-off neighbourhoods, their dwellings were on relatively big plots compared with Britain. Here in the UK, where the average house price is £200,000 at the time of writing, you'll struggle to get the space you want. To me space equals quiet, which equals rest, which equals contentment.

I don't need to hear the neighbours' arguments or drunken kids on a Friday night going up the road shouting and screaming and smashing up whatever they can. That's not what I moved in to *Torywood* for!

Another thing that annoys me is travelling on an overcrowded tube first thing in the morning. There I'll be, my head studiously buried in

Who knows but God, just what **opportunities** or appointments we sometimes **miss** in our **hurry** to look after **number one**?

a book – *any* book – so long as I don't have to interact with anyone. Someone is strap-hanging a few centimetres away, whose armpit I will wash *and* shave, if it gets any closer. Heaven knows they need it! To my left is a gentleman who looks like he's eaten absolutely all the pies in London's pie and mash shops. He's making his way towards me. 'Please God, please God, don't let him sit here, please!' He squeezes one buttock, and then somehow miraculously the next, into the seat on my left before saying, 'Turned out nice again!' The fact we're now hurtling along London's Underground rail network hundreds of feet below normal life has obviously escaped him.

He's invaded my personal space. Finally, I escape the confines of my grubby metal tomb and surface, blinking at the daylight around me. I'm on Oxford Street where crowds of people swarm all around me. The hustle and bustle of the pre-Christmas shop is underway.

Then it hits me. In my own selfish desire to protect *my* precious environment, I might have entertained an angel unawares. I could've talked to him and responded to his opening remark – instead of glowering and grunting. Who knows but God, just what opportunities or appointments we sometimes miss in our hurry to look after number one?

Perhaps he was lonely and needed to talk.

Now I'll never know.

NICK'S NOTES THINGS TO DO

✔ MAKE TIME

✔ MAKE SPACE

✔ MAKE ROOM FOR OTHERS

28

BOOTY CALL

It might just be my age, but when I used to watch pop videos or music programmes on TV, they weren't that shocking. Now and again on *Top of the Pops*, you might witness a cameraman being a little overzealous. When the dance icons Pan's People performed, occasionally the lens would follow them a little too closely but that was about it, really. Nothing too risqué.

Now I feel like I have to **edit** all the **music** channels before my kids watch them. On some stations, it's like (and I'm really sorry to have to say this) soft porn for teenagers. Young women bump and grind their way around, wearing what passes for a postage stamp on their bottom half and a couple of tea bags on their top. The camera follows their every tiny move, while their male counterparts grab their crotches and try to look tough – *and yet* sensitive and sexy – all at the same time. If it wasn't so sad, it might be hilarious.

But it's not.

It's a booty call. Coming to a screen near you. Sending all the wrong messages about moral values, dress codes, gun law, inappropriate behaviour and sex. Trying to sell what appears on the screen as normal. No wonder the youth are confused. There's nothing quite so funny as two middle class kids trying to speak the language of the ghetto:

'Word up my blood w'happen with mi homework?'

I'm off to get a blue rinse and read up on Mary Whitehouse

'No worries itz all safe man. Brup. Innit?'

This is not Compton. This is Chorleywood.

It's a booty call. But it has nothing to do with Wellingtons or beauty as far as I am concerned. As for me, I'm off to get a blue rinse and read up on Mary Whitehouse. Now there was a woman who was ahead of her time!

NICK'S NOTES THINGS TO DO

✔ BUY A PROFESSIONAL EDITING SUITE AND CUT OUT ALL THE NAUGHTY BITS FROM THE WEEK'S TV PROGRAMMES

✔ THEN WATCH THE 3 MINUTES THAT ARE LEFT

29

RECYCLING

Over the past few years I've become green. No, not with envy. But with the desire to invest in the future of this fragile planet God has given us. I'm trying to be a better steward of its resources.

Over the **past few years** I've become **green**

For years I've been filling our precious atmosphere with all sorts of aerosols, carbon emissions and other noxious gases. At one point in the late nineties, I possessed a Jeep Grand Cherokee. This massive monster truck guzzled petrol at an alarming rate and cost £60 a time to refuel (who knows how much it would cost now?). Happily for me, if not for the environment, it wasn't my money.

You don't have to be a rocket scientist to realise the type of weather and seasonal changes we've been used to for most of our lifetimes are becoming a thing of the past. And the changes occurring mean the weather is a lot more extreme.

Is it too late to do anything about it? Are we shutting the stable door after the horse has bolted? Well, I think perhaps, yes. Because until we can get the biggest polluters on this planet to sign up to a greener way of life, I think we'll be a little like King Canute sitting on his throne . . . while the water slowly and inevitably floods all around him.

But what can we do?

Well, there are practical steps such as buying fair trade and green products, recycling our cardboard, garden waste, glass, paper and tin, buying cars with smaller engines, maybe the next one might even be electric . . . saving water and all that. But I also think we should lobby our politicians on behalf of our generation, and more importantly future generations: our children and grandchildren. What kind of legacy do you want to give them?

As always, pray that people's minds would be transformed on this issue. Pray that the leaders of the countries who are the biggest culprits would change their minds, too – *and* do something positive and world changing. Very soon.

I know this, though. If we do nothing, we'll have failed to be responsible stewards of God's precious creation. Everyone can make a difference – no matter how small. Every little bit helps.

What God created, let's not destroy out of ignorance, laziness or fear. Let's harvest the good, the clean, the green, the desirable and the precious.

If we do **nothing, we'll** have **failed** to be responsible stewards of God's **precious** creation

We may plough the fields and scatter the good seed on the land.
But it is fed and watered by God's almighty hand.

NICK'S NOTES THINGS TO DO

✔ RECYCLE AS MUCH AS I CAN

✔ TRY NOT TO USE THE CAR TO GO TO THE
SHOPS

✔ GET A WATER BUTT

✔ GET A SMALLER BUTT!

30

WHERE DOES YOUR HEART RESIDE?

'Wherever your treasure is, there the desires of your heart will also be.'
(Jesus – as remembered by the apostle Matthew, Matthew 6:21)

A few years ago, a well-known songwriter came to my house. I was about to drive him to Yorkshire to work with one of the Spice Girls collaborators.

Rich in earthly terms
– perhaps not in others

'Where do you live?' my wife inquired.

'Well, I have a house in Cuba,' he replied, 'an apartment in Belgravia, and a place near Mijas in Spain. But I spend most of my time in California.' He then went on to list the rest of his properties around the globe.

We were left wondering if he ever managed to feel settled anywhere. He appeared to be a musical nomad. Rich in earthly terms – perhaps not in others.

Back in the early nineties, I was in Berlin just after the wall had fallen. I was with a colleague from Radio 1, helping him to check out the city prior to a broadcast from there. Coincidentally, a legendary seventies rock band whose album I'd been charged with promoting also happened to be in town. And not being one to look a gift horse in the mouth (or anywhere else for that matter), I arranged for my colleague to interview the band later that night after their show at the Enormodrome, or whatever it was called.

It was late. Things with one of the band members got more than a little philosophical. He pointed at his girlfriend and said, 'Yeah, she used to be a Christian. But she's come over to our side, now.' The sudden turn in conversation freaked me out.

Later that night I sat up in bed, praying for wisdom and protection – and also that God would win her back. I felt ill prepared, and to some extent ambushed. I wondered, where does her heart reside? Had she really given up, worse still, crossed the line?

Are you caught up in the money pit – knocking yourself out week after week trying to make ends meet? Are you striving to achieve greatness in your particular field? Are you longing for recognition? Give it up. God knows your needs and desires. He sees everything, right down to the last detail.

What we need to do is surrender – and pray through everything with praise and thanksgiving.

Where does your heart reside?

God knows your **needs** and **desires** He sees **everything** right down to the last detail

NICK'S NOTES THINGS TO DO

✔ MONITOR MY HEART

✔ WHO DOES IT BEAT FOR?

31

OUTWARD BOUND

'Remain faithful to what you have been taught from the beginning'
(The apostle John, 1 John 2:24)

I've just signed a series of forms committing my daughter to the Duke Of Edinburgh's award scheme. She'll boldly go up hill and down dale, camping, climbing, serving – and hopefully growing through this process. It's something she wants to do. I'd be lying if I said I wasn't a little nervous.

My friend and I shared a **dormitory** with a bunch of lads from the **wrong side** of the tracks in Glasgow

As a young man aged 13, I went on an outward-bound course at Aviemore in Scotland. My friend and I shared a dormitory with a bunch of lads from the wrong side of the tracks in Glasgow. I got to see how people from less fortunate backgrounds lived. It opened my eyes.

I climbed Ben Macdui with a team of adults, went white water canoeing and capsized, and sailed on Loch Morlich where a storm blew up out of nowhere. I was mightily relieved to see my parents at the end of the week. They in turn noted how grown up I'd become. I was outward bound alright.

In nature, the tiny sparrow is nurtured and fed by its mother. But there comes a time when it's urged to leave the nest – to see if it can fly and enjoy its own freedom and responsibilities.

We bumble through life while our heavenly daddy – who loves us more than we can possibly know – watches over us

So it is with our children. For the mother, I think that process can start as early as when the child first goes to school, then perhaps college, university – or the first day they start work. I believe it's a process which for us parents never, ever stops. That is, until we die. My dad is 76 now, and he still looks out for me. I can imagine being the same with my children.

However, there's a balance between letting go and holding on too tightly. Nobody likes to feel suffocated or hemmed in. But it's painful as a parent to have to watch your kids make mistakes. You can pray with them, listen to how they feel their days have been, give them a cuddle when they need it, and go above and beyond the call of duty. Yet still, somewhere, no matter how perfect a parent you think you are, they'll still make mistakes. And it'll be painful. We have to be there to scoop them up and help them get on with life. They're outward bound, finding their way. It's all new, uncharted territory.

So it is with us and God. We bumble through life while our heavenly daddy – who loves us more than we can possibly know – watches over us. Sometimes he'll grieve about the scrapes we get ourselves into but he'll always be there to pick us up, comfort us and plant our feet back on the right path.

For now we're outward-bound. But one day we'll be coming back home.

NICK'S NOTES THINGS TO DO

✔ MAKE A LITTLE MAP, SHOWING WHERE MY DAUGHTER WILL BE GOING ON HER EXPEDITION

✔ PRAY THAT SHE HAS FUN AND THAT THE TRIP IS SUCCESSFUL

32

THE BEAUTIFUL GAME

I am 6 years old, standing in the freezing cold with my father and our next-door neighbour who keeps shouting, 'Up the Owls.' I have no idea why he keeps doing this, as I can't see any birds – feathered or otherwise – in sight.

I do know that in an instant, I've fallen in love. I'm at Hillsborough watching Sheffield Wednesday playing the mighty Reds – Manchester United. My dad, who is a proper Mancunian and therefore a City fan, can't bring himself to shout the odds for United. So he doesn't say much apart from when Wednesday score when he lets out a mighty 'Yes!' It doesn't happen often enough though, and Man Utd. win comfortably.

I do know that in an **instant** I've fallen in **love**

I've been treated to a masterful display by the likes of Sir Bobby Charlton, Denis Law and the late and much missed George Best – among many other great players – Paddy Crerand, Willie Morgan,

Bill Foulkes, Alex Stepney and the fearless Nobby Stiles. From that day forward I've been hooked.

My favourite year in the past 43 of following my beloved team has to be 1999 when we won the treble. That – and the time Ryan Giggs ran past most of the Arsenal team to put the ball in the back of the net. That was a moment to savour, etched deep into my memory! So what was it exactly that inspired my initial passion?

I think it was a combination of things. The atmosphere, the strongly tribal – and at times almost primal – feeling and the sense that I was largely among men. There was much banter, a lot of humour and singing. Mostly songs about the referee and who his dad was. And there was a great sense of occasion. There was no violence. In fact, if anything, you looked after each other. I only got frightened once as in the aftermath of the game I felt I was getting lost in the mêlée leaving the stadium. Then two arms linked either side of mine and I was lifted floating with the crowd until it was safe to put me down. What a day! A red letter one.

Years later, at 40, I started playing once a week. My mind was agile and would tell my body to spin on a sixpence, strike the ball first time with my right foot and put it in the back of the net. My body steadfastly refused to do as it was told. I would stay rooted to the spot or swing wildly at it, just about connecting with the ball only to see it go sailing over the bar.

My spiritual life has sometimes felt a bit like that. When I first became a Christian, I was massively enthused. As the years have gone by, and life – like a decent defender – has tried to kick the living essence out of me, my faith has been tested. If I'm really honest, I've felt like giving God two yellows and a red.

I never have but I've come close. Now I know that spiritually I'm not in the flush of youth, and I haven't got the speed or grace of Ronaldo, but you wouldn't want to try getting past Roy Keane when he was at the top of his game now, would you? He was possibly one of the greatest midfielders of all time but has gone into management, looking after Sunderland. I, too, am on the move as I want to become a writer and a broadcaster, a communicator of my faith. I sincerely hope God blesses me with more skills than he did on the football field. I have a funny feeling I'm going to need them.

> I sincerely hope **God blesses** me with more **skills** than he did on the **football field**

Love football. Love life. Love God.

NICK'S NOTES THINGS TO DO

✔ PRACTISE THE GAME

✔ PLAY THE GAME

✔ FINISH THE GAME WELL

33

LONG DIVISION

One of the most painful things to witness in any church or organisation is dissension and division. It's often brought about in all innocence simply through poor communication and management skills. Then if the rumour mill starts to fly, what was perhaps a simple oversight can become misunderstood and blown out of all proportion.

what was perhaps a simple oversight can become misunderstood and blown out of all proportion

That's when the body count can begin. The first symptoms can be seen in the giving from church members which can drop dramatically. If left unchecked, the numbers on the electoral role will also diminish over time. The vicar and his family are the first in the firing line, and will often suffer great pain as a result. But why does this happen?

Well, I think it's down to a couple of things. First, if we upped our giving and the church was properly funded, vicars and pastors alike could be paid a living wage. That might help. But I also think we need to spend less time gossiping – and more time praying and listening.

It's a peculiarly British trait that we seem to build people up only to knock them down when they make a simple human error, or we think they've got too big for their boots. And that's a great shame.

I also think we expect far too much from our clergy and their families. I think the established churches are slow to embrace change but the fact is that Christianity as we know it in the UK is on the decline. We have to move with the times – and not stay with our feet firmly planted in the last century.

what kind of society do we want our children and grandchildren to grow up in?

And change is painful. But in my experience, it can also be a valuable way of growing. If we truly want to 'stand up for Jesus' and evangelise this nation, it will not be comfortable. It will require the courage of not just the few but also the many.

Let's ask ourselves this: what kind of society do we want our children and grandchildren to grow up in?

We've been too docile, too liberal and too lazy for too long. If we remain in this languor and flaccidity, the church will atrophy – and maybe our faith with it.

NICK'S NOTES THINGS TO DO

✔ MAKE SURE I'M LOVING THE VICAR AND HIS FAMILY

✔ PRAY FOR STRUGGLING CHURCHES THAT I KNOW

✔ BE THANKFUL FOR HEALTHY CHURCHES

34

TEACHERS

'My mates went to university. I went on the road and experienced the university of life. I graduated with a first class honours in 'Hindsight'. It cost me a lot more than a grant.'

(Nick Battle)

Everyone has memories of their favourite, and least favourite, teachers. I had this head of year, who we'll call Jack South. He was a big smoker. His skin resembled a man who had a definite appreciation of the sun – as well as tobacco.

Everyone has **memories** of their **favourite,** and least favourite, **teachers**

He had a funny speaking voice and also facial ticks – which I now realise might have been due to Parkinson's or a similar disease. It would've been easy for us all to extract the proverbial from him. But he was funny.

He had an authority about him and quietly commanded respect. He was also a wonderful listener. Later, he provided a sympathetic ear when I was in the sixth form, harangued by my fellow prefects for squandering my academic future on an imaginary musical career. He was wise, yet he was firm.

My least favourite was the deputy head of the junior school I went to as a child. He was a bully who resorted to corporal punishment. At any given opportunity, he'd whack

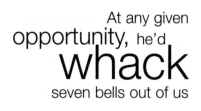

At any given opportunity, he'd **whack** seven bells out of us

seven bells out of us, running a regime of fear. Fuelled by his outbursts and our failure, I hated his lessons. The angrier he got, the more afraid we were. Our work suffered – which only served to pour more fuel on the fire.

It's my experience that a good teacher will spot the potential in a child. And that teacher will do his or her best to foster encouragement in their particular subject. They will help students achieve their potential.

And so it is, I believe, with our heavenly father. He sees our potential. He longs to see our lives – and those of others – transformed by the power of his Holy Spirit. He watches us grow and mature in his love, so we may share it with others.

This is the gift of teaching, of being a mentor, someone who can encourage and guide, listen and advise. Watch and pray.

Teachers . . . on the whole I love 'em.

NICK'S NOTES THINGS TO DO

✔ AM I A MENTOR TO SOMEONE WITHOUT REALISING IT?

✔ I MUST GO AND POLISH MY PREFECT'S BADGE

✔ I MUST GO AND POLISH UP ON MY MENTORING

35

ARCHIE HALL

I had my first drink as a toddler. My mum would give me a teaspoon of whisky to help me sleep when I had measles as a 3-year-old. Much later, I progressed from underage beer drinking to relaxing with a glass of wine at the end of the day.

Then I became a record promoter. I used to spend every lunchtime wining and dining radio and television producers. Drinking started to mean a little more. I was in my early thirties, though, and didn't really notice too much of a down side. However, if I'd had a drink at lunchtime, by 6 o'clock my body would be craving sugar – and I could be a little grumpy.

I used to spend every lunchtime wining and dining radio and television producers

At various points I've completely cut out alcohol. But I came to rely on it when my wife was in the late stages of her cancer – and then after her death.

Once I'd opened a bottle of wine, I'd struggle to stop. It's a pattern that's continued right up to this very day. It's responsible for my being overweight and having high cholesterol. That means taking statins. On top of all that comes sleep apnoea. That means I have a little machine pumping air into my lungs to stop my airways from collapsing every night. I look like a cross between Darth Vader and Dennis Hopper in the film *Blue Velvet*.

I'm 50. It's 10 years since my mum died of alcoholic dementia at 66. You'd think I'd be able to wake up and stop.

But I struggle.

> I also know **I shouldn't be in bondage** to anything or anybody

I know all the biblical arguments. Give beer to those who are perishing. Take a *little* wine for your stomach's sake.

I also know I shouldn't be in bondage to anything or anybody. I guess I feel this is the last and most powerful stronghold that our spiritual enemy has over me. Genetic maybe. Emotional and manipulative. Certainly.

Do you have a similar problem? Chocolate? Porn? Narcotic? Finance? Sex? Whatever it is, we're commanded to do something about it. For me, just for today, I'm going to take a small step and try and opt for fruit juice tonight – as opposed to my usual libation.

I'll keep you posted.

NICK'S NOTES THINGS TO DO

 KEEP THE WINE FIRMLY IN THE CELLAR!

36

TRUST

'Don't put your trust in mere humans.
They are as frail as breath. What good
are they?'
(Isaiah, prophet, Isaiah 2:22)

Trust is a difficult thing to gain, built up over time but eroded in a second. I trust that my wife and children love me. But that's borne out on a daily basis by the way we live together and love each other.

Having teenage daughters teaches you much about trust. You trust they'll go to a party, have a wonderful time, and not do anything they'll regret later. However, I find it extremely difficult to trust their male counterparts. To me, they look less like gentlemen – more like a pack of scavenging hyenas!

> Having **teenage daughters teaches** you much about **trust**

We trust the government will look after our best interests yet they lost the data to a huge percentage of the country's homes – complete with the details of child support and our bank accounts that the money is paid into.

It beggars belief that such sensitive information could 'disappear' in the twenty-first century. Yet it has. A laptop or a disc suddenly goes missing – and we're talking about much more than a few music downloads here. Such gross incompetence leaves me breathless.

What constitutes a breach of trust or an abuse of privilege? Take, for instance, the married teacher who dates a teenage girl, later setting up home with her. Did his wife trust him? Did the girl's parents trust him – or would they rather he'd never entered their lives, or anything else, for that matter?

We look up to people in positions of authority – church leaders, government, police and armed forces and our bosses at work. We trust them to do the right thing. Are we right to do so – or incredibly naïve?

It's one thing to put our faith and belief in God. But to invest too much in man and woman, when we all know how fallible we are . . . that's another matter.

We look up to people in positions of authority

I believe trust and respect of our fellow humans is earned. It should not be given blindly because of a person's power, position or title. The more you're given in this life, the more responsible and accountable you need to be. I believe the Bible backs this.

What we should do is put our faith and trust in God, while always looking for the best in everyone. We all disappoint from time to time. But God never does.

NICK'S NOTES THINGS TO DO

✔ DON'T FOCUS ON PEOPLE

✔ DO FOCUS ON GOD

✔ ALL THE TIME

37

VISION

When everything put together falls apart, what can we do? When our community seems to be crumbling, how should we respond? When someone claims to either hear the voice of God or know where they think the Holy Spirit is taking the rest of us, I find it hard to challenge them. Why? Well, I'd never dare to claim such a thing. It feels almost audacious to me. And yet historically, people have clearly been able to do just that. I tend to see God's purposes worked out over time when I look back at things and can see what he has done. Yes, it's important to have dreams, hopes and ambitions but at some point all these have to be given back to our maker. We can talk about a gift from God, but we should never, ever, let that gift become so important that we forget about the giver.

So if God truly gives you **a vision,** keep it – and him – **in perspective**

So if God truly gives you a vision, keep it – and him – in perspective. I'm reminded of a line from the song 'Muscle Culture', by my old band mate the late great Steve Fairnie from Writz – 'I have a vision, a tele-vision . . .' He was gently chiding the televangelists of the seventies.

I'm not trying to trivialise or belittle the men and women of God who claim these things. What I'm trying to say is, let's be really careful what we claim. Look deep for discernment. Hold it all lightly. Don't let the gift become bigger than the giver.

In our excitement at what the Lord is doing – or what we think he's doing – we mustn't lose perspective. We must keep testing it out. We must continue to be faithful in prayer. We must stay humble and seek advice from our elders – wise, spiritual, older men and women – who may have a valuable insight that we may have missed.

We must stay **humble** and seek **advice** from our **elders**

Let's not let a 'good idea' blind us from the greatness of God and the mercy and loving kindness he wants for us all.

NICK'S NOTES THINGS TO DO

✔ DO LISTEN TO PROPHETS

✔ DON'T LET THEM PROFIT FROM YOUR LISTENING

38

HIGH ANXIETY

'Such love has no fear, because perfect love expels all fear.'
(John, the apostle, 1 John 4:18)

So many people are **plagued** by worry

So many people are plagued by worry. They walk around with stomachs knotted up in fear. They examine everyone, including themselves, in minute detail. They're anxious for everything to be right and in its proper place. They wake in the night hours. Their minds won't let them rest. Cogs whirr. Heart and brain speed into action to test, torment and terrify.

You don't have to be a professional, paid-up exorcist to come to the grand conclusion that this is the devil's playground. There are few things the enemy likes more than to taunt, divide and bring trauma to the soul. Division and hatred are his oxygen. Derision and anger his lifeblood.

We mustn't give him room to operate. When you're a Christian standing up for your beliefs, then you become – as my friend Mark Stibbe would say – a TRE (Target Rich Environment). That doesn't mean we have to walk around paranoid, constantly looking over our shoulder. It does mean we have to be properly equipped: 'Put on all of God's armour,' writes the apostle Paul, 'so that you will be able to stand firm against all strategies of the devil' (Ephesians 6:11).

To fail to do this is like setting sail in a force 10 gale across the English Channel in a dinghy without a life jacket. Expect to drown. Only the mighty hand of God can still the ocean and in his mercy pluck us from our stupidity.

But there's a problem. We're human. We mess up. So what can we do? It's not easy. It has to start when we repent, say sorry and have the courage to start again. For some of us that's a daily occurrence. For the rest of us . . . we're either incredibly blessed or incredibly 'economical with the truth'.

Stop worrying. Start living. Today is a brand new day. God is the harbinger of joy and giver of second, third, fourth chances. Live as you were meant to live, in fullness of joy, filled with the Holy Spirit and walking with him.

Don't be crushed by the dictator of fear. Stand firm in the knowledge that God is omnipotent, omniscient and omnipresent.

Only the mighty hand of God can still the ocean and in his mercy pluck us from our stupidity

NICK'S NOTES THINGS TO DO

✔ DON'T WORRY, BE HAPPY

✔ . . . BECAUSE GOD IS MY STRENGTH

39

BUTTERFLIES

'An old man may be a babe in Christ, and a young person can be spiritually mature.'
(Dr Martyn Lloyd-Jones)

What was God up to when he made butterflies? They're such beautiful creatures yet according to some people they live tragically short lives. Frequently, they get trapped inside conservatory windows and shed doors on glorious summer days. And then spend most of their time exhausting themselves, trying to escape.

I've known people like that. They've blazed a trail like a comet through my life, providing incendiary excitement and glamour. They self implode or disappear off the face of this earth all too soon.

However, as one dear friend of mine says, 'It's better to put life into your years than years into your life.' And, to an extent, I think he's right. I don't want to spend my latter years in a rocking chair, mumbling quietly to myself just waiting for God to take me.

So not for me the butterfly and its brief, mythical fleeting visit. Or, for that matter, the rocking chair and a steady stream of health care professionals. Somewhere between the two lies the balance. Only God knows when and how the scales will tip – and in whose favour.

Let's just hope he's in a good mood on the day in question.

NICK'S NOTES THINGS TO DO

✔ DON'T STAY IN A ROCKING CHAIR FOR TOO LONG

✔ DON'T GET TRAPPED BEHIND A SHED DOOR

✔ DO KEEP MOVING

40

LUVVIES

You'll find luvvies in all sorts of places. But their natural habitat is theatre and television. Highly charged and very emotional, these creatures can be insecure, often excruciatingly funny, sometimes confused and camp as a row of tents. They'll emit, moan and groan in pursuit of their art, going to remarkable lengths. They're normally wonderful all-rounders who can sing, dance and act – sometimes all at the same time.

They can **carp** and **bitch** with the **best of them**

They can carp and bitch with the best of them. But if ever a fellow thespian is in need, they'll run to their aid offering tea and generous amounts of sympathy, and a wonderfully well-rounded shoulder pad to cry on. They understand fellowship. Even if it's only for a brief run while cast and crew are together, it provides a colourful family environment.

It's like that touring with various bands – as I have done over the years. As soon as the first gig was over, we'd get into the 'tour bubble'. Here was safety, a phalanx of phantasmagorical talent moving around from town to town, country to country. Here within the bubble, a band of brothers and sisters would often behave in a way that would never be considered appropriate in the real world.

Relationships would develop, reach deep levels of love and understanding – and then crash and burn as soon as the tour/show was over. Often in-jokes and a whole other language would be spoken. If you were part of the bubble, it was fine. But it could be a prickly and sometimes embarrassing experience for friends and relatives coming to visit who would try and converse. A little luvvies club.

Luvvies mean well. But if they were to carry on inveterately, in time they'd become extinct. They might *talk* a lot about procreation – who did what to whom – and how often. But when the show's over, they're 'simply too tired to do it, darling!'

church can be a little 'luvvies club'

Similarly, church can be a little 'luvvies club'. Its rituals and language are foreign and uncomfortable for anyone visiting for the first time. However, Jesus' club is meant to be inclusive. In fact, it's the only club in the world that exists solely for non-members. When he turned over the tables in the area of the Temple reserved for Gentiles, he expressed genuine anger at what people had done to his Father's house. We shouldn't be afraid to do the same thing where appropriate.

NICK'S NOTES THINGS TO DO

✔ REMEMBER TO TALK TO VISITORS AT CHURCH

✔ INVITE THEM ROUND FOR A CUP OF TEA AND SLICE OF CAKE

✔ PUT THEM AT THE TOP OF THE LIST FOR HOSPITALITY

41

THE FINE ART OF FORGIVENESS

As Christians we can talk a good game. We can trot out all the right Bible verses. We can say all the right things. But when it comes to forgiveness, honesty and integrity – and trying to put all of them into practice – I find them to be the hardest things in life.

But when it comes to forgiveness. . .

I can remember about 10 years ago, being with a young work colleague in Dublin checking out a music festival. We'd had a good night, it was late and I was anxious to get my kip. So imagine my dismay when I got into bed to find he'd emptied the entire contents of an ice machine into the bottom of it. To say I was apoplectic with rage would be an understatement. I was incandescent!

. . . I find them to be the **hardest** things in **life**

I rang his room, remonstrated with him on the spot, questioned who his father was, his sexual habits and many other things besides . . . before climbing back on to what had now become my 'water bed'.

The next morning, in my unforgiveness, I hatched a plan. Six months down the line it was finally birthed in the middle of the Arizona desert at our company's conference. As it was my young colleague's first conference, I thought I'd wind him up a bit. While he was having breakfast, I broke into his room, nicked all four jackets he'd brought with him, and left him a ransom note. If he wanted to see his clothes again, he had to be in the bar at 7 p.m. and bring $100 in cash. Later that morning we were sitting next to each other. He showed me the note I'd written.

'This is class,' he said, 'a quality wind-up. Who do you think did it?' At this point I had the opportunity to come clean. Instead I said something else.

'I think it's Jon from the American company – he's always good for a laugh.'

That afternoon, my colleague broke into Jon's room while he was out playing golf. He stole the entire contents of his mini-bar (some $300 worth), leaving him just one solitary beer. Then he came to tell me the news and what he'd done. Still I steadfastly refused to confess. Later, as I handed out his jackets to four female staff members, I was beside myself with mirth.

That evening at 7 o'clock on the dot, my mate turned up in the bar and then at 5 minute intervals, so did the girls. It was very funny – but probably not very kind and certainly not forgiving. Not only that, it escalated further when one of our team booked an alarm call for 4 a.m. for the entire party to go snipe hunting. There were lots of very grumpy people later that day – and no snipe anywhere to be seen.

Unforgiveness leads to resentment, which brings its own actions and consequences.

Unforgiveness leads to resentment, which brings its own actions and consequences

As I write, I'm wrestling with an issue of unforgiveness in my heart. I know I'm commanded to love the person – even if I hate what they've done. I also know that at 50, I should know better. But we don't always and that can cause us, and others, more pain than we need.

So I'm going to try. If God can forgive me for all the slime in my life, I should be big enough to do the same for anyone else who wrongs me. Time to dive deep into the well of salvation and cling to the promise given to us.

NICK'S NOTES THINGS TO DO

✔ BREATHE IN DEEP

✔ TELL MYSELF THAT FORGIVENESS IS A LIFESTYLE

✔ JUST DO IT

42

THE GODFATHER

Last night I stood in a twelfth century church at a tiny Northamptonshire village. I watched my 13-year-old godson being confirmed, as he publicly acknowledged Jesus through his own choice, for the first time.

> I felt at times like I'd walked onto the set of *The Vicar of Dibley*

The service was old-fashioned, full of 'thou, thy, shalt and shalt nots'. Yet there was a quiet humility and faithfulness about it all. The bishop was lovely, and the lady vicar had a quiet radiance about her.

The organist must have been in her eighties, but was also a marvel to behold as she stirred the freezing cold organ into life to play 'Be Still And Know'. Any more 'still' and I think we would have frozen. If you were lucky enough to be under one of the radiators, you got a glimmer of warmth. However, if you were not in close proximity, then it was bracing to say the least. I felt at times like I'd walked onto the set of *The Vicar of Dibley*.

It was a Wednesday night. It was the middle of a busy week in the run-up to Christmas. Yet the church was full, as the community came together to worship God and celebrate the communicant's decision to follow Christ.

As one body, we shared communion. Even though the body of our Lord tasted like rank polystyrene and the wine like Ribena, it was still a blessed time. Sometimes when you're embroiled in a big and seemingly successful 'Spirit-filled church', with amazing preaching, music that rocks your socks off and youth pastors who are incredibly committed, it can be easy to be a little disdainful about smaller, humbler churches. Like the church last night, they may be steeped in tradition, not have one worship song less than 30 years old and can also be freezing cold. Yet for us – God was present. He was present in the lives of the young and old making their precious commitment. He was present in the service of the frail 80-year-old woman on the organ. He was present in a community coming together to celebrate.

I experienced **meekness, humility and grace**, quietly without pomp

I experienced meekness, humility and grace, quietly without pomp. I also experienced love. Not to mention a huge lump in my throat as the bishop laid his hands on my godson's head. I prayed that the power of the Holy Spirit would be with him all the days of his life.

I am a godfather. But it can't stop there. How can it? It's a whole new beginning.

Well done, Hugh! And thank you, Jesus.

NICK'S NOTES THINGS TO DO

✔ DON'T CONDEMN CHURCHES FOR THEIR LACK OF ROCK AND ROLL

✔ DO COMMEND CHURCHES FOR THEIR LACK OF POMP AND CEREMONY

✔ HAVE A GREAT TIME WHEREVER GOD IS PRESENT

43

ONE HUMP OR TWO?

Sometimes it's the little things in life that create the most stress – the straw that breaks the camel's back.

You may have been carrying some information or knowledge about someone or something, and it's weighing you down like a ball and chain. Sometimes I sincerely wish that people would not choose to share their treasures of darkness with me, as I don't always feel equipped to cope with what they download. And the graphic details and nuances of their deeds or thoughts cloud my brain and worry my already over-taxed heart.

At other times, I just feel incredibly flat, like nothing will make me smile

At other times, I just feel incredibly flat, like nothing will make me smile. Ever felt like that? But how do we cope when we're feeling jaded, run of the mill, or just plain sad?

Well, one of the most common mistakes is to indulge oneself in over-eating, drinking too much, shopping too much, even (though this is certainly not true in my case) exercising too much. All of which will make you feel good for a while. But later you can feel weighed down with responsibility and regret.

'A problem shared, is a problem halved,' my mum used to say. Well, that maybe true. But what if you can't share the information for reasons of confidentiality? The only place to take it to is the foot of the cross. And it is here we must lay everything down. For good. Having done that, don't pick it up, or keep running back to see how it's doing. Try your best to leave it there and ask your heavenly father to help you when you feel you can't cope anymore.

> Then, with all your might, **throw** it into the **water** (mind the ducks!)

Try a practical expression of this deep mystery. Go to a beach, or a lake, and find a stone. With the stone in your hand, speak out your grievance as if transferring all that angst into the stone. Then, with all your might, throw it into the water (mind the ducks!). Your burden is now in the deepest sea (or pond).

It's my personal experience that God won't let you down, and you will come through. Walking in faith and by his grace.

NICK'S NOTES THINGS TO DO

✔ GIVE IT ALL TO GOD

✔ KNOW THAT HE HEARS ME

✔ REST IN HIS PEACE

EPILOGUE

(or the bit at the end)

So that was *The Daily Male* – what started out as a daily rant and rave to God is now in your hands. Thank you for getting this far and I pray that you've been amused but most of all blessed.

GRAVEL ROAD MINISTRIES
– our aims

- For Nick to give his testimony and lead people to Christ.

- To stand with and pastor the bereaved, particularly those with young families.

- To mentor musicians, songwriters and worship leaders.

For further information please contact:

Nick Battle
PO Box 375
Chorleywood
Herts
WD3 5ZZ

gravelroadministries@mac.com
www.nickbattle.com
www.philotrust.com
www.authenticmedia.co.uk

NICK BATTLE

Big Boys Don't Cry

The autobiography
of Nick Battle

Nick Battle Soaking In The Spirit

Let Go & Let God